Lecture Notes
in Business Information Processing 528

Series Editors

Wil van der Aalst, *RWTH Aachen University, Aachen, Germany*
Sudha Ram, *University of Arizona, Tucson, AZ, USA*
Michael Rosemann, *Queensland University of Technology, Brisbane, QLD, Australia*
Clemens Szyperski, *Microsoft Research, Redmond, WA, USA*
Giancarlo Guizzardi, *University of Twente, Enschede, The Netherlands*

LNBIP reports state-of-the-art results in areas related to business information systems and industrial application software development – timely, at a high level, and in both printed and electronic form.

The type of material published includes

- Proceedings (published in time for the respective event)
- Postproceedings (consisting of thoroughly revised and/or extended final papers)
- Other edited monographs (such as, for example, project reports or invited volumes)
- Tutorials (coherently integrated collections of lectures given at advanced courses, seminars, schools, etc.)
- Award-winning or exceptional theses

LNBIP is abstracted/indexed in DBLP, EI and Scopus. LNBIP volumes are also submitted for the inclusion in ISI Proceedings.

Dimitri Petrik · Andrey Saltan ·
Andreas Helferich

Editors

Digital Product Management in the Era of Data Economy, Artificial Intelligence, and Ecosystems

First International Conference
on Digital Product Management, ICDPM 2024
Gothenburg, Sweden, June 12, 2024
Proceedings

Springer

Editors
Dimitri Petrik 🆔
University of Stuttgart
Stuttgart, Germany

Andrey Saltan 🆔
LUT University
Lahti, Finland

Andreas Helferich 🆔
International School of Management (ISM)
Stuttgart, Germany

ISSN 1865-1348   ISSN 1865-1356 (electronic)
Lecture Notes in Business Information Processing
ISBN 978-3-031-71514-3   ISBN 978-3-031-71515-0 (eBook)
https://doi.org/10.1007/978-3-031-71515-0

This Springer imprint is published by the registered company Springer Nature Switzerland AG
The registered company address is: Gewerbestrasse 11, 6330 Cham, Switzerland

If disposing of this product, please recycle the paper.

Preface

Welcome to the proceedings of the 1st International Conference on Digital Product Management (ICDPM 2024). This conference was co-located with the Digital Product Management Week held in Lindholmen Science Park in the vibrant and knowledge-intensive city of Gothenburg, Sweden. The Digital Product Management Week was held from June 10th to 14th, and the International Conference on Digital Product Management was held on June 12th, 2024.

The conference brought together researchers and practitioners to explore the theme "Digital Product Management in the Era of Data Economy, Artificial Intelligence, and Ecosystems" and exchange cutting-edge research results on the evolution of software product management. This evolution is determined by the increasing share of data-driven products and the integration of artificial intelligence, digital services, and digital artifacts co-created in ecosystems. Accordingly, the conference aimed to foster critical exchange on the issues attributed to this change. In particular, the conference was interested in research about data-driven startups and the agility required in processes and strategies for data-centric business models that differ from traditional software business models.

The Digital Product Management Week was initiated by Jan Bosch (Director of the Software Centre at Chalmers University) and Helena Holmström Olsson (University of Malmö). In addition, the International Software Product Management Association (ISPMA®), an open, non-profit association of experts, researchers, and industrial professionals fostering excellence in managing software products across industries, joined in the organization of the conference.

Andreas Helferich (ISM Stuttgart), Dimitri Petrik (University of Stuttgart), and Andrey Saltan (LUT University) were responsible for the scientific part of the week. The conference was also organized with the great support of the Management of Application Development and Maintenance (WI-MAW) expert committee of the Gesellschaft für Informatik (German Informatics Society) and the associated Software Product Management (WI-PrdM) expert group, of which Andreas Helferich and Dimitri Petrik act as speakers.

The conference sees digital product management from the intersection of business and software engineering perspectives. In doing so, we understand digital management as a scientific discipline as well as an operational function in our software-driven world. In addition, the decision to collaborate with the Digital Product Management Week was driven by the wish to foster exchange with practitioners and digital startups. Our conference chairs see the dissemination of knowledge and challenges between academia and practice as one of the distinctive characteristics of our conference.

The following conference proceedings incorporate the accepted research papers that were presented at the conference. We received 19 submissions and decided to accept seven papers (one short paper and six full papers) after a double-blind peer review process. Our organizational team is delighted to announce that with the help of our program committee members, we have succeeded in providing three reviews for each submission.

The submissions cover a wide range of timely issues in digital product management. Helena Holmström Olsson and Jan Bosch explore the necessity for companies to advance from software agility to system agility. Based on evidence from the embedded systems domain, the authors propose a formula for determining optimal release frequencies for digital products. Nasreen Azad and colleagues perform a thematic analysis of critical success factors in adopting DevOps techniques and practices. The paper offers 16 propositions and organizes them in a theoretical framework. Wolfram Pietsch researches digital product sustainability, emphasizing trade-offs between conflicting goals. To manage these trade-offs the paper conceptualizes a balanced approach that follows the principles of Quality Function Deployment. Vitor Mori and Hans-Bernd Kittlaus introduce a context-aware framework for managing software platforms as internal products within IT organizations, emphasizing the adjustments needed in requirements management and release planning to improve organizational competitiveness and agility. Yevgen Bogodistov and colleagues report the results of a discrete choice experiment concerning the perceptions of the micro-credential software ecosystem by higher education institutions. The authors investigate how micro-credential ecosystems change decision-making in higher education institutions and redefine the educational landscape. Based on a literature review, Nan Yang and colleagues conceptualize the emerging 6G ecosystem, discussing the antecedents, components, and consequences of a 6G ecosystem. Philipp Hofer and Georg Herzwurm analyze how European cloud providers can turn the challenges posed by cloud sovereignty into market opportunities by developing business models based on trustworthy and legally compliant cloud solutions which are distinctive to the offerings from US cloud providers.

In addition to the presentation of these seven papers, the event offered lots of thrilling talks. Below is just a snippet of the program. Niclas Nygren's keynote on Volvo Cars' data strategy highlighted the importance of treating data as a product and the role of data governance in accelerating analytics. Luka Crnkovic-Friis from King (the company behind Candy Crush) shared how AI and machine learning are transforming product development and productivity at King, a company that was data-driven from the very beginning but which is drastically changing the way they do business currently. Pekka Abrahamsson analyzed the impact of generative AI on digital product management and demonstrated a loop of intelligent agents interacting with each other and refining digital products in multiple cycles. The event also offered workshops, such as the one moderated by Miroslaw Staron, Jan Carlson, and Kristian Sandahl, which ignited discussions about software engineering in a post-generative AI world. The variety of topics was meaningfully enriched by a startup roundtable, a summer school for doctoral researchers, and a poster session by Software Center Gothenburg.

We want to thank everyone involved in organizing the conference and contributing his or her latest research work. In particular, we want to thank the authors and speakers for enriching the program, as well as the program committee for the comprehensive reviews, the keynote speakers for exciting talks, and the local organization team, led by Malin Rosqvist, who made ICDPM 2024 possible.

We appreciate the interesting topics and many exciting discussions between academics and practitioners!

June 2024

Dimitri Petrik
Andrey Saltan
Andreas Helferich

Organization

General Chair

Andreas Helferich International School of Management, Stuttgart

Program Chairs

Dimitri Petrik University of Stuttgart, Germany
Andrey Saltan LUT University, Finland

Program Committee

Andreas Oberweis Karlsruhe Institute of Technology, Germany
Benedikt Krams Match Rider, Germany
Christian Kop University of Klagenfurt, Germany
Christopher Hoppe Fraunhofer-Institut für Software- und
 Systemtechnik ISST, Germany

Dominik Siemon LUT University, Finland
Eckhart Hanser DHBW University, Germany
Frederik Möller Technische Universität Braunschweig, Germany
Georg Herzwurm University of Stuttgart, Germany
Gero Strobel Universität Duisburg-Essen, Germany
Hans Brandt-Pook Bielefeld University of Applied Sciences,
 Germany

Hans-Bernd Kittlaus InnoTivum, Germany
Helena Holmström Olsson Malmö University, Sweden
Hendrik van der Valk TU Dortmund, Germany
Jan Bosch Chalmers University, Sweden
Jürgen Münch Reutlingen University, Germany
Karin Vosseberg Hochschule Bremerhaven, Germany
Katharina Peine highQ Computerlösungen GmbH, Germany
Krzysztof Wnuk Chalmers University, Sweden
Lars Mautsch STACKIT, Germany
Malin Rosqvist RISE, Sweden
Martin Engstler Hochschule der Medien, Germany
Martin Mikusz DHBW Stuttgart, Germany

Masud Fazal-Baqaie	Next Data Service, Germany
Nane Kratzke	Lübeck University of Applied Sciences, Germany
Ralf Kneuper	IU International University of Applied Sciences, Germany
Sami Hyrynsalmi	LUT University, Finland
Thorsten Schoormann	Technische Universität Braunschweig, Germany
Thorsten Spitta	Bielefeld University, Germany
Wolfram Pietsch	Aachen University of Applied Sciences, Germany
Xiaofeng Wang	Free University of Bozen-Bolzano, Italy

Cooperation Partners

Contents

Towards Business Agility 2.0

Helena Holmström Olsson[1]([⊠]) [ID] and Jan Bosch[2] [ID]

[1] Malmö University, Malmö, Sweden
helena.holmstrom.olsson@mau.se
[2] Chalmers University of Technology, Gothenburg, Sweden
jan.bosch@chalmers.se

Abstract. Business agility is key for companies across industry domains. As a primary mechanism for achieving agility, agile development practices have been successfully adopted by software organizations. However, while agile practices successfully support software agility, business agility also requires system agility. For companies in the embedded systems domain, this is particularly challenging since business agility is achieved only when all technologies in the system, i.e., mechanics, electronics, software, and artificial intelligence (AI) are subject to agile cycles. Although there is prominent research on business agility, industrial best practice shows that effective adoption of these frameworks is scarce. As a result, agility remains at primarily a software level. In this paper, we focus on companies in the embedded systems domain and ways in which these companies can increase system agility. The contribution of the paper is two-fold. First, we identify the limitations of contemporary agile frameworks. Second, we define a quantitative approach for determining the optimal release frequencies for the different technologies that are part of an embedded system.

Keywords: Business agility · system agility · software agility · embedded systems · release frequency

1 Introduction

Business agility is critical for competitive advantage and refers to rapid, continuous, and systematic adaptation to customer demands, market dynamics and changing business environments [1–4]. Agile development practices are portrayed as one of the primary mechanisms for achieving business agility. By emphasizing close customer collaboration and iterative development in short sprints, agile practices enable software teams to increase responsiveness and shorten development cycle time [5]. However, for a business to be agile, the entire system needs to be agile. For companies in the embedded systems domain, this means that software agility needs to be complemented with agile cycles that allow continuous improvement of mechanics, electronics, and artificial intelligence (AI). As one of very few examples of this, Tesla recently announced a chip upgrade that provides existing car models with self-driving capabilities [6, 7]. While no Tesla cars are fully autonomous yet, the upgrade of this electronics component reflects the opportunity to enhance system capabilities with upgrades that go beyond software. Despite an

D. Petrik et al. (Eds.): ICDPM 2024, LNBIP 528, pp. 1–14, 2025.
https://doi.org/10.1007/978-3-031-71515-0_1

impressive number of frameworks for how to scale software agility, however, examples of system agility are few. As a result, agility remains at a software level and resides within the software part of the organization. At heart, business agility is a challenge for product management. This function needs to decide how to realize business agility in the system design, how to exploit its capabilities as well as focusing efforts on topics that customers care for and can be monetized.

As business is hardest to realize in companies in the embedded systems domain, this is where we focus our attention. We explore the attempts these companies pursue to increase the scope of agility with the intention to move from software to system agility. The research question we explore is the following: *How can system agility be understood in the context of embedded systems and how can we help ensure that the value embedded systems companies generate is higher than the costs involved in their agile development and deployment cycles of different components?*

The contribution of the paper is two-fold. First, we identify the limitations of contemporary agile frameworks and the implications of these limitations in practice. Second, we define a quantitative approach for determining the optimal release frequencies for the different technologies that are part of an embedded system. The remainder of the paper is organized as follows. In Sect. 2, we review literature on agility. In Sect. 3, we describe the research method. In Sect. 4, we summarize our empirical findings. In Sect. 5, we identify the limitations of contemporary agile frameworks. In Sect. 6, we define a quantitative approach for how to determine the optimal release frequencies for the different technologies in an embedded system. In Sect. 7, we conclude the paper, and we outline future research.

2   Background

Business agility is critical to a company's ability to survive and thrive in a turbulent market [8, 9]. While the concept of agility is not new, the digital transformation that companies across domains makes it only more important [10]. What we experience is a shift towards digital businesses with continuous development, deployment, and monetization of customer value [11]. In such a business landscape, agility is key. For companies in the embedded systems domain, business agility is achieved only when all technologies in the system are subject to agile cycles. However, although there is prominent research on how to achieve business agility, industrial best practice shows that companies still struggle with extending agile practices beyond software. Below, we review literature that illustrates how agility has been successfully implemented at a software level but that examples of system agility are few.

2.1   Software Agility

Agile development methods are the primary mechanism for achieving agility in software development. With methods such as e.g., Scrum, Kanban, Extreme programming (XP) and Crystal, companies adopt a lean approach to software development [12]. Although the methods differ in techniques and tools, they share the common characteristics of incremental and adaptive development [12–15]. During the last decades, the initial focus on one, or a few, agile teams has shifted to large-scale agile development [12]. To support this, several frameworks for how to scale agile practices has been introduced with SAFe, LeSS, DAD, Nexus, Scrum of Scrum and the Spotify model being some of the most common ones [16, 17]. Similarly, practices such as DevOps, DataOps and MLOps, seek to unify development teams with functions such as operations, data analytics and machine learning model training [18–20] to facilitate continuous connection of these competence areas.

2.2 System Agility

Embedded systems are systems that encompass hardware as well as software components and that has a dedicated function within a larger mechanical or electrical system [22]. Despite attempts, examples of agility at a system level are few. Due to its nature, mechanics and electronics components are not easily upgraded and although most embedded systems companies are mature when it comes to software agility the same is not true for system agility [21]. As one of very few industry examples on how to successfully scale agile beyond software, Tesla recently offered its customers a Full Self-Driving (FSD) chip upgrade [6, 7]. With this electronics upgrade, existing car models are provided with enough power to allow for fully self-driving cars when the software catches up. In addition, Tesla offers a hardware retrofit in which model 3 buyers with the FSD software bundle get a hardware 2.5 to 3.0 retrofit with a simple service center appointment. While examples like these are few, they illustrate the way in which the ability to upgrade system functionality allows for continuous improvement of product value.

2.3 Agility in the Embedded Systems Domain

Typical embedded systems are cars, aircrafts, telecommunication systems, video surveillance systems and wind turbines etc. During the last two decades, companies in the embedded systems domain have adopted agile practices within their software organizations and they are deploying software on a frequent basis using DevOps practices [23, 24]. These companies are experiencing a rapid transformation of their conventional businesses due to digitalization [10, 11]. This implies that to stay competitive, embedded systems companies need to master not only software agility but also system agility. To achieve this, these companies need mechanisms that help them understand the optimal release frequency for all technologies in the system. In addition, they need support that help them ensure that the value they generate with each release exceeds the costs involved for development.

2.4 Summary: Software, System (and Business) Agility

Previous research shows on successful examples of agility at a software level. However, there are only very few examples where embedded systems companies work with non-software components, as well as AI components, in an agile fashion. In Fig. 1, we summarize how agility is implemented at a software level, how there are only few examples of agility at a system level and how agility has not yet been successfully expanded to also include the business level in embedded systems companies.

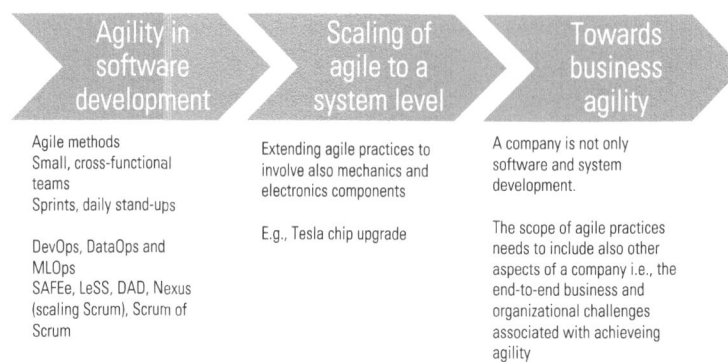

Fig. 1. Agility at a software, system, and business level.

In what follows, we report on research in which we help companies achieve system agility. We do so by developing an approach for determining the optimal release frequencies for the technologies in an embedded system with the intention to help companies reason about value versus costs in continuous, and agile, improvement of systems.

3   Research Method

3.1   Research Context and Approach

The research presented in this paper is part of a larger research initiative in which we conduct longitudinal multi-case study research [25, 26], in close collaboration with companies in the embedded systems domain. Within this context, we initiated this research by inviting all companies with an interest in business agility to a workshop series consisting of four online workshops. The companies cover domains such as telecom, automotive, industrial embedded systems, defense, security/surveillance, energy etc., and with the common characteristic being that the systems they develop include technologies ranging from mechanics and electronics to software, data and artificial intelligence (AI). All companies struggle with how to evolve non-software components, how to determine the optimal frequency of upgrades and how to balance cost versus value gained of different technologies. These are all critical aspects of business agility but still, aspects that are not empirically explored. We adopted a qualitative research approach [26, 27], as this approach is well-suited for studying organizational contexts.

3.2   Case Companies

The case companies develop software-intensive systems such as cars, trucks, security cameras, vessels, defense equipment, manufacturing plants, and water pumps. In Table 1, we detail the number of companies and the number of people attending each of the workshops we organized. The workshop series were initiated in September 2020 and the four workshops were run in a sequence with each workshop focusing on a specific aspect of business agility and how to achieve this. In each workshop, we had a mix of companies representing the different domains. When referring to the companies in the findings section of this paper, we group them according to the domains they represent. Our reason for this is that we see that companies within the same domain typically share a set of common characteristics. The domains we refer to is *automotive, telecom, industrial embedded systems, defense, energy and security/surveillance.* In the workshops, we had company representatives in roles ranging from agile coaches and Scrum masters to product owners, product and portfolio managers, technical specialists and data scientists. In three of the workshops, we also had people from purchase, sales and from units involved in marketing and customer-facing activities. As the criteria for selection of workshop participants, we reached out to our key contacts at each company to ask them to identify the people they found most relevant for the topic and question at hand. This resulted in workshops with highly relevant people in key roles for driving the adoption of agile practices within each company. It should be noted that although the workshops series constitutes the primary data source for this research, we have engaged with the companies for more than a decade. During these years, the topic of agility has been key to our research on continuous integration, continuous delivery, data driven development and digital transformation, see e.g., [28–31].

Table 1. The number of companies and people attending the workshops.

	Workshop I	Workshop II	Workshop III	Workshop IV
Total number of companies	9	6	10	10
Total number of people	28	10	22	24

3.3 Data Collection and Analysis

All workshops were online workshops, held in English and they lasted for 3–5 h. During the workshops, the two researchers shared the roles of facilitating the workshop, documenting the discussions, taking pictures and responding to questions. During all workshops, notes were taken to capture the group discussions and any illustrations that were shared were documented. Also, all companies were asked to share a short presentation in which they presented e.g., challenges and opportunities they experienced in relation to the topic at hand. After each workshop, the slides from these presentations were shared with the researchers and with the group to provide additional empirical data and to enhance knowledge sharing among the companies. All workshop notes were shared between the researchers to allow for further elaboration and analysis of the empirical material.

During analysis, we adopted an interpretative approach [26, 27]. Following this approach, we revisited the documentation from all workshop discussions to carefully reflect on our insights from these and what implications could be drawn from the empirical material. In this process, all workshop notes were read with the intention to identify recurring elements and concepts [32]. In addition to the workshops, our findings build on frequent communication and informal meetings with key stakeholders, continuous e-mail and phone interactions, participation in online company events and presentations.

3.4 Validity of Results

To ensure validity of results [25], and to address *construct validity*, we started each workshop with presenting our definition of software and system agility. In this way, we could discuss alternative interpretations already before we ran into potential misunderstandings. With respect to *external validity*, the approach we define in this paper was derived based on our experiences from embedded systems companies in six domains. To address external validity, we used our empirical cases to inductively derive our findings with the intention to provide value for companies that have common characteristics as the companies we studied. All case companies involved in this study are in the embedded systems domain. Consequently, the guidance we provide is of primary relevance for companies in this domain. However, our findings might also provide value in domains with similar characteristics as the ones we studied. Finally, to address reliability, we applied established practices for data collection and analysis, and we made sure our results were frequently reviewed and approved by company representatives.

4 Findings

4.1 Agile Software Organizations

The case companies involved in our study develop and deliver safety-critical systems consisting of mechanics, electronics, software, and AI components. During the last decade the software parts of the systems have rapidly increased in size and from being an activity that was either outsourced or taken care of by external consultancy firms, software development has become a critical in-house activity. As part of building in-house software organizations, the case companies have successfully adopted agile practices. Many of them use a DevOps approach to enable frequent delivery of software to customers. To introduce agile practices, most companies started with a few agile "pilot projects" to explore new ways-of-working, create best practices and have people familiarize with techniques and tools. In one of the companies developing industrial embedded systems, the manager describes: *"Five projects were selected to run as agile "pilot projects" as a start. In these, instead of doing the complete project before delivering products to the customer, small series were made very early in the project and feedback was used to adjust the technical scope. After the real product release, feedback was used to decide which new features should be added to the product."* Another company in this domain started the agile initiative by introducing a new development system based on lean and agile principles. As emphasized by one of the agile coaches in the company, the system *"...does not only belong to methods and processes (team level) but also to managers at the business level that help drive the adoption and bring agile "to life"."* Common in all case companies is that the adoption of agile practices has brought new measures into the organizations. They all seek to shorten cycle time and improve innovativeness and therefore, metrics such as e.g., project cycle time and number of new products are collected across the organizations. Still, they report on difficulties when it comes to monitoring customer value and ensuring that new features add the value they are intended to produce.

4.2 Agile Beyond Software

Traditionally, any changes to mechanics and electronics components have been both costly and time-consuming and regarded as an activity you try to avoid. In one of the automotive companies, the major obstacles are the need for process equipment, the high costs associated with this equipment and the long lead times of anything non-software. In addition, there are surrounding factors that make things at a system level more complex as is reflected upon by one of the project managers in one of the automotive companies: *"There are support functions such as compliance, patent, technical marketing etc., that are not fully allocated or dedicated to the project which often means that the given task might not be prioritized. In addition, dependencies from platforms that are serving several projects make things difficult."* Another company reports on similar challenges when describing the organization as highly component-driven and with difficulties in integrating the different functions. The need for a more systems-driven organization is clear but the diverse product portfolio and large number of product variants make common ways-of-working as difficult as a common architecture. Still, this company is pushing for continuous improvement of hardware with e.g., change or reconfiguration of an axel as something that is already achieved. Here, equipment like press tools set limitations on cycle time and speed and one of the product managers explains how *"...we adapt based on the expensive equipment we have to maximize the use of these."* In continuing, this company representative describes how: *"We are moving towards a situation where we think in terms of more continuous improvement also outside software. We need the possibility to change things and we can do this using simulations and 3D printing techniques as this decrease costs."* Still, scaling agile beyond the software organizations prove difficult and the case companies struggle with historically strong silo organizations, different technologies requiring different expertise, functions such as portfolio, HR, sales etc., that are not used to agile methods.

In addition, new digital technologies prove almost as challenging to involve in agile cycles as many of the traditional technologies. As an example, all case companies develop systems in which AI components are becoming increasingly common. Across domains, machine learning (ML) models are integrated into the systems allowing capabilities such as e.g., image recognition, autonomous driving, predictive maintenance, error prediction, speech recognition, connectivity security etc. While the opportunities with these technologies seem endless, the development, training, deployment and retraining of these models challenge current ways-of-working. The experience in the case companies is that contemporary agile frameworks provide very limited support for how to scale agility to involve these technologies.

4.3 From Traditional Towards Digital Businesses

The companies involved in our study experience a situation in which the systems they produce are complemented with digital technologies and where innovation efforts are increasingly taking place in software and AI. While this by no means implies that the mechanics and electronics components are not as critical as before, it means that these, as well as the associated expertise, need to rapidly adjust and integrate with new technologies. As one example, the automotive domain foresees a future in which the electrification of cars will dramatically reduce the need for traditional maintenance. Consequently, the revenue in this area will drop. In this company, the strategy going forward is to experiment with different business models to identify new revenue streams. As described by one of the technical experts in the company: *"The market is changing rapidly, and the traditional revenue streams are no longer the only ones or the most viable ones. We used to earn money on metal pieces, and we still do, but there is additional revenue in for example the data we generate, and we need to learn how to best capture it."* With regards to agility, the companies realize that the on-going digital transformation puts increasing demands on their business processes, practices, and revenue models. To accommodate this, and to align expectations, the case companies need the ability to improve system components in similar ways as those they already practice in relation to software. And while they all agree that the agility of software teams is indeed a start, they do recognize that they need more than this to stay competitive.

4.4 Summary: Software and System Agility

To summarize our empirical findings, we provide a mapping in which we show the maturity of the different company domains with regards to software and systems agility. The maturity levels we use are the following: unaware, aware (not employing), initiating/running pilots/experiments, partially adopted (employed in parts of the system) and fully adopted. These maturity levels were derived based on the insights that the company representatives shared with us, and they reflect to what extent agility is employed at a software and/or system level. For each maturity level, we use a color coding indicating to what extent the different domains have achieved software and/or system agility. We use 'black' for software agility and 'grey' for system agility (Fig. 2).

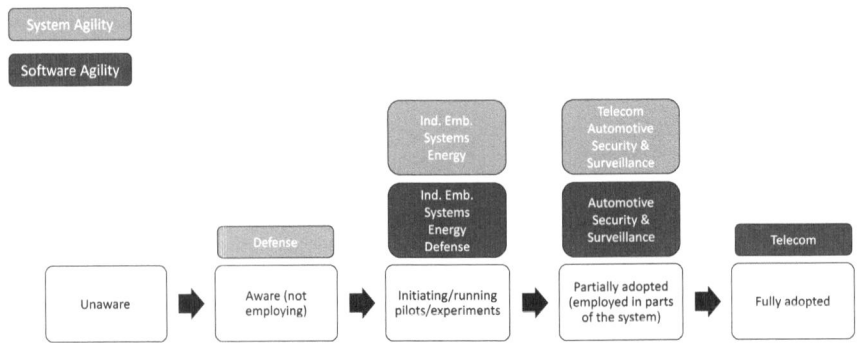

Fig. 2. Mapping of the maturity of the company domains with regards to software and system agility.

5   Key Limitations of Contemporary Agile Frameworks

Based on the challenges that the case companies experience, we identified several limitations in contemporary agile frameworks such as e.g., [12, 16, 17] and similar. Below, we describe these limitations, and we detail the implications these have on the case companies.

Contemporary agile frameworks stay within reactive definitions of agility, i.e., a focus on being 'responsive', 'cope' and 'survive' change. For the companies, this means that they lack effective and hands-on support for how to proactively initiate, drive and accelerate change.

Contemporary agile frameworks provide little support for large embedded systems that involve technologies ranging from mechanics and electronics to software and AI. While software is developed and delivered in continuous and rapid cycles other system components are not. As a result, there is insufficient support for systems with non-software components that play a critical role as enablers for the system to function.

Contemporary agile frameworks fail to effectively involve functions outside software. All case companies report on challenges with involving functions such as marketing, purchase, sales, HR, and general management in agile cycles. Therefore, the benefits of agility remains primarily within the software organization.

Contemporary agile frameworks prove difficult to apply in practice. Despite available methods, processes and tools, functions outside software are difficult to align and hence, agility doesn't scale.

Contemporary agile frameworks fail to recognize that companies operate in a dynamic environment with continuous cycles and with feedback loops within each of these cycles. Instead, they often assume that organizations operate in a "I am in a steady state – something happens –I respond" scenario. For the case companies, this means that the frameworks they use provide only limited support.

6   Towards a Quantitative Approach for Determining Release Frequency

Below, we identify the factors that impact the value generated by new system functionality. Also, we present a generic formula that help companies ensure that the value they generate is higher than the costs involved in development and deployment of the different components in their systems.

6.1   Factors

Below, we list the key factors that impact value creation and capture:

Customer value (V_c): Customer value is understood as the perception of what a specific product or service is worth to a customer in relation to possible alternatives.

Value capture percentage ($V_{c\%}$): Value Capture indicates the percentage of the value provided to customers that is captured by the company itself.

Development cost (C_D): Research and development (R&D) costs relate to the research and development of a company's goods or services, as well as any intellectual property generated in the process.

Manufacturing, distribution, and installation cost (C_{MDI}): For physical components, such as mechanical and electronic parts, there are cost involved in the manufacturing, distribution, and installation of new versions of these components in systems in
the field. This is different from digital components that are basically free to distribute
and install.

Certification cost (C_c): Safety-critical systems where a failure can result in accidents
with fatal or high cost consequences, need to certify their products as per domain-
specific safety standards. Similarly, for industries where regulatory compliance is critical,
evidence trails need to be maintained continuously and certification of each release of
system component may be required.

Number of instances (N): Some of the costs discussed in this section, such as
development and certification cost, can be amortized over the system instances affected
by a new release of a component. Other cost, such as the manufacturing, distribution
and installation cost need to be carried for each individual system instance.

6.2 Generic Formula

Based on the factors outlined, there is the opportunity to calculate the value generated,
as well as the costs involved, in development of functionality. Below, we present a
quantitative approach with which we seek to help companies ensure that the value they
generate is higher than the costs involved.

$$V * V_\% \geq (C_D + C_C)/N + C_{MDI}$$

Fig. 3. Generic model for calculating optimal release frequency for a component.

As show in Fig. 3, the optimal release frequency for any component, independent of
the technology, is defined by the value generated for the company and the cost incurred
for realizing the new version of a component. The value part generated for the company
is the result of two factors. First, the amount of value generated for the customers (V).
The more value an updated and improved version of a system component provides to
the customers, the higher this factor will be. The second factor is the percentage of the
generated customer value that the company providing the component can capture from
its customer base ($V_\%$). It should be the ambition of any company to deliver as much
value as it can to its customers. However, this does necessitate a business model that
allows the company to capture sufficient value for itself to cover costs. The cost part of
the equation consists of three main factors. First, there is the cost of development (C_D).
For all technologies, there is a cost associated with development of a new version of
the component. Second, there may be cost for certification (C_C) in the case of safety or
regulatory requirements. These costs need to be amortized over all the system instances
(N) receiving the new version of the component. The third cost is concerned with the
manufacturing, distribution, and installation cost (C_{MDI}) of the component. For software,
this cost tends to be 0 or very close to it, but obviously this is not the case for electronical
and mechanical components. The optimal release frequency of a component is where
the result of the formula in Fig. 3 is equal or larger than 1. In this case, the value for the

company associated with the release of a new version of a component exceeds the cost of the release. The costs shown in Fig. 3 show why the frequency of software releases tends to be much higher than the frequency of releases of new electronic or mechanical components. Also, it clarifies why releases of components, including software, that need to be certified tend to be less frequent.

6.3 Instantiation for Embedded Systems Technologies

Below we instantiate the formula for each of the different technologies in an embedded system, In the case of reinforcement learning (RL), deployed systems engage in online retraining of AI models without human involvement. In this case, the RL algorithm learns from its own successes and mistakes and, over time, improves its performance. As is shown in Fig. 4, instantiating the generic model for a RL case results in the following:

$$V * V_\% \geq (C_D)/N$$

Fig. 4. Model for calculating optimal release frequency for a reinforcement learning (RL) component.

On the cost side, there is only the initial development cost of developing the RL model and deploying it. On the value side, the same factors remain. However, unless the company providing the system can capture value from the improved performance of the system due to RL, there is no point for the company to provide this functionality. To illustrate this, an automotive company could deploy a RL model to allow the engines in its vehicles to experiment with improving fuel efficiency. However, today these companies lack a business model that allows them to capture part of the benefits resulting from improved fuel efficiency. This lack of business model than causes this to be not pursued in practice as no monetary incentives exist. However, a company operating a robot-taxi operation would most certainly want to use this RL model as it would, potentially significantly, reduce its operating cost.

In the typical case of development of software using a DevOps approach, the generic model can be instantiated as shown in Fig. 5:

$$V * V_\% \geq (C_D + C_C)/N$$

Fig. 5. Model for calculating optimal release frequency for a software component.

Here, the cost includes the agile teams as well as, where required, the cost for software certification. As an example, the telecom case company releases new software to systems in the field on a bi-weekly basis. This generates significant value for the company and its customers. In this case, however, there is no certification cost associated with software releases which makes the release process less expensive. For electronic and mechanical components, the generic model shown in Fig. 3 applies completely. The main factor is the necessity of certification of new component versions as these costs are often high.

Here, the most illustrative example is the FSD chip upgrade provided by Tesla [6]. For these customers, the new chip makes possible for software functionality that the previous chip didn't have the capabilities to run. Also, some of our case study companies have started preparing for continuous improvement of electronic and mechanical components. The challenge with these components, however, is that these tend to be more of an enabling nature. For example, the FSD chip upgrade provides additional computational capabilities that only become valuable when these capabilities are used by software features and AI models that provide the actual value for customers. Another example can be found in the defense industry. In this domain, most systems are expected to have a functional life of 30 years with a mid-life upgrade after 15 years. As the defense industry is now also exploring continuous deployment of software, this means traditionally that companies had to install very expensive, bleeding edge technology to allow for sufficient headroom for 15 years of operations. The industry is now, however, starting to understand that is much cheaper to install mainstream hardware in its products and to conduct more frequent, e.g. every 3–5 years, upgrades of mainstream electronics. This allows the industry to exploit the power of Moore's law available to civilian industries.

7 Conclusions

In this paper, we report on multi-case study research in which we identify the limitations of contemporary agile frameworks. Based on our findings, we define a quantitative approach for determining the optimal release frequencies for the different technologies involved in an embedded system. Our approach involves a set of factors that impact the value generated by new system functionality. We capture these factors in a generic formula that help companies ensure that the value they generate is higher than the costs involved in development and deployment of functionality. In future research, we aim to focus on the business agility dimension and detail the transition from system to overall business agility including business model and continuous value capture aspects.

References

1. Baškarada, S.: The Seven S's of Organizational Agility. AWS Cloud Enterprise Strategy Blog, 11 March 2021
2. Tsourveloudi, N.C., Valavanis, K.P.: On the measurement of enterprise agility. J. Intell. Rob. Syst. **33**(3), 329–342 (2002)
3. Haeckel, S.H.: Adaptive Enterprise: Creating and Leading Sense-and-Respond Organizations. Harvard Business School Press, Boston, Massachusetts (1999)
4. Dove, R.: Response Ability – The Language, Structure, and Culture of the Agile Enterprise. Wiley, New York, New York (2001)
5. Abrahamsson, P., Warsta, J., Siponen, M.T., Ronkainen, J.: New directions on agile methods: a comparative analysis. In: Proceedings of the 25th International Conference on Software Engineering (ICSE), pp. 244–254. IEEE Computer Society, Washington, DC, USA (2003)
6. https://www.theverge.com/2019/7/8/20685873/tesla-fsd-chip-upgrade-2019-install-hw2-full-self-driving. Accessed 16 Apr 2021
7. https://www.eetasia.com/teslas-hardware-retrofits-for-model-3/. Accessed 16 Apr 2021

8. https://www.linkedin.com/pulse/business-agility-vs-organizational-same-ronald-ross/. Accessed 16 Apr 2021
9. Mathiassen, L., Pries-Heje, J.: Business agility and diffusion of information technology. Eur. J. Inf. Syst. **15**(2), 116–119 (2006)
10. Mathiyalakan, S., Ashrafi, N., Zhang, W., Waage, F., Kuilboer, J.P., Heimann, D.: Defining business agility: an exploratory study. In: The Proceedings of the 16th Information Resource Management Association International Conference, San Diego, CA, 15–18 May 2005
11. Olsson, H.H., Bosch, J.: Going digital: disruption and transformation in software-intensive embedded systems ecosystems. J. Softw. Evol. Process, e2249 (2020)
12. Bosch, J., Olsson, H.H.: Digital for real: a multi-case study on the digital transformation of companies in the embedded systems domain. J. Softw. Evol. Process, e2333 (2021)
13. Dingsøyr, T., Nerur, S., Balijepally, V., Moe, N.B.: A decade of agile methodologies: towards explaining agile software development. J. Syst. Softw. **85**, 1213–1221 (2012)
14. Abrahamsson, P., Warsta, J., Siponen, M.T., Ronkainen, J.: New directions on agile methods: a comparative analysis. Paper presented at the 25th International Conference on Software Engineering, Portland, Oregon (2003)
15. Cao, L., Ramesh, B.: Agile software development: ad hoc practices or sound principles? IT Prof. **9**(2), 41–47 (2007)
16. Rajlich, V.: Changing the paradigm of software engineering. Commun. ACM **49**, 67–70 (2006)
17. https://www.scaledagileframework.com/organizational-agility/. Accessed 16 Apr 2021
18. Salameh, A., Bass, J.M.: Spotify tailoring for architectural governance. In: Paasivaara, M., Kruchten, P. (eds.) XP 2020. LNBIP, vol. 396, pp. 236–244. Springer, Cham (2020). https://doi.org/10.1007/978-3-030-58858-8_24
19. Munappy, A.R., Mattos, D.I., Bosch, J., Olsson, H.H., Dakkak, A.: From ad-hoc data analytics to DataOps. In: Proceedings of the International Conference on Software and System Processes, pp. 165–174 (2020)
20. Ebert, C., Gallardo, G., Hernantes, J., Serrano, N.: DevOps. IEEE Soft. **33**(3), 94–100 (2016)
21. John, M.M., Olsson, H.H., Bosch, J.: AI on the edge: architectural alternatives. In: Proceedings of the 46th Euromicro Conference on Software Engineering and Advanced Applications (SEAA), pp. 21–28. IEEE (2020)
22. Bosch, J., Olsson, H.H., Crnkovic, I.: Engineering AI systems: a research agenda. In: Artificial Intelligence Paradigms for Smart Cyber-Physical Systems, pp. 1–19. IGI Global (2021)
23. Heath, S.: Embedded Systems Design. EDN Series for Design Engineers, 2 edn. Newnes (2003)
24. Leite, L., Rocha, C., Kon, F., Milojicic, D., Meirelles, P.: A survey of DevOps concepts and challenges. ACM Comput. Surv. (CSUR) **52**(6), 1–35 (2019)
25. Zhu, L., Bass, L., Champlin-Scharff, G.: DevOps and its practices. IEEE Softw. **33**(3), 32–34 (2016)
26. Kaplan, B., Maxwell, J.A.: Qualitative research methods for evaluating computer information systems. In: Anderson, J.G., Aydin, C.E. (eds.) Evaluating the Organizational Impact of Healthcare Information Systems, pp. 30–55. Springer, New York, NY (2005). https://doi.org/10.1007/0-387-30329-4_2
27. Walsham, G.: Interpretive case studies in IS research: nature and method. Eur. J. Inf. Syst. **4**(2), 74–81 (1995)
28. Dybå, T., Prikladnicki, R., Rönkkö, K., Seaman, C., Sillito, J.: Qualitative research in software engineering. Empir. Softw. Eng. **16**(4), 425–429 (2011)
29. Olsson, H.H., Bosch, J.: The five purposes of value modeling. In: Proceedings of the Euromicro Conference on Software Engineering and Advanced Applications (SEAA), 26–28th August, Slovenia (2020)

30. Holmström Olsson, H., Bosch, J.: Data driven development: challenges in online, embedded and on-premise software. In: Franch, X., Männistö, T., Martínez-Fernández, S. (eds.) Product-Focused Software Process Improvement. LNCS, vol. 11915, pp. 515–527. Springer, Cham (2019). https://doi.org/10.1007/978-3-030-35333-9_36
31. Fabijan, A., Dmitriev, P., Olsson, H.H., Bosch, J.: Effective online experiment analysis at large scale through SegVis. In: Proceedings of the 19th International Conference on Product-Focused Software Process Improvement, PROFES (2018)
32. Ståhl, D., Mårtensson, T., Bosch, J.: Continuous practices and DevOps: beyond the buzz, what does it all mean? In: Proceedings of the 43rd Euromicro Conference on Software Engineering and Advanced Applications (SEAA), pp. 440–448 (2017)

Balancing the Sustainability of Digital Product Management from a Strategic Business Perspective

Wolfram Pietsch[(✉)]

Department of Business and Economics, FH Aachen - Aachen University of Applied Sciences,
62068 Aachen, Germany
pietsch@fh-aachen.de

Abstract. The sustainability of digital products is not limited to ecological aspects. From a strategic perspective, ecological as well as social and economic aspects are important. From a comprehensive understanding of sustainability, continuity in general is concerned, including product development and management itself. Sustainable digital product management should integrate the perspectives of the customer, the technology and the company and also pursue different sustainability strategies. From a strategic perspective, internal and external resources as well as corporate functions and temporary tasks should be balanced. In order to evaluate the feasibility of QFD-based approaches, a flexible QFD-based framework for strategic and operative sustainability deployment, a specific example of a comprehensive strategic deployment for digital product management and an analysis of goal trade-offs regarding sustainability are devised.

Keywords: sustainability · software development methodology · QFD · product management · business strategy · user needs · utility of requirements · balanced scorecard · strategy deployment · goal trade-offs

1 Sustainability and Digital Product Management

1.1 Strategies for Comprehensive Sustainability

As the public and academic awareness of sustainability grows, research and practice are increasingly focusing on relevant topics, including the development of IT products. Sustainability research in information systems has been focussing on ecological aspect (green IT) primarily [1, 2]. In classical engineering, durability has been always a primary issue and a measure for quality. The durability of software is not a primary issue in software business and academia. Some discussions concerning technical measures, customer integration and business models may contribute to the idea of lasting software, but there is neither broad theories nor techniques dedicated to sustainability from a strategic perspective [3, 4].

There is some research on the impact on economic aspects, i.e. on the impact on business models [5, 6]. From a strategic perspective on sustainability, environmental

D. Petrik et al. (Eds.): ICDPM 2024, LNBIP 528, pp. 15–27, 2025.
https://doi.org/10.1007/978-3-031-71515-0_2

and business aspects should be integrated with social aspects into a 'triple bottom line' [7, 8] for any product development. This has been postulated as a research agenda for information systems recently as well [9]. 'Triple bottom play' may be a good as a rhetoric claim, but not for an operationalisation of sustainability [10].

The concept of sustainability must be defined more specific. There are many different definitions of stainability which have been incorporated in a **comprehensive definition of sustainability** postulating that.

- "after a defined period of time, (…)
- a program (…) and/or implementation strategies continue to be delivered and/or (…)
- individual behaviour change (…) is maintained;
- the program and individual behaviour change may evolve or adapt while (…)
- continuing to produce benefits for individuals/systems." [11]

How about the sustainability of digital product management? Following the comprehensive definition, digital products should continue to be delivered, meaning that digital products should be employed over a defined period of time. The behaviour change going along with the usage of digital products should keep on during this period of time and may change withholding (or changing) its benefits for the user and/or organisation. Hence sustainable digital products should not be designed by predefined and static requirements, they may evolve but should keep delivering benefits to the user.

Classical product development methodologies are driven by the specification of requirements which are defined as "capabilities needed by a user" [12]. Users are a source but not the subjects of analysis. There is an increasing societal demand for sustainability but it is not sufficient to include sustainability issues which are felicitated relying on the awareness of the user. Hence it is not sufficient in terms of sustainability to enquire the user hoping for sustainability needs: there are tacit or implicit needs which at least some customers are not aware of or which are conflicting with other needs such as convenience. Furthermore, there are sustainability goals of the business which are conflicting with individual needs of users leading back to the triple bottom line from a birds-eye perspectives.

Modern, agile development methodologies are flexible to changes but delegate the responsibility for the continuing delivery of value to the product owner for the 'period of time' during the development of the product. Then a product manager might take over with a change in perspective and goals. If not, the product may degenerate in terms of sustainability, which conforms to common-sense in product management practice. Which program or strategy would be suitable for sustainable product management from the creation to the discontinuation of products? It should be flexible and keep the focus on continuing benefits to the customer considering the changes of goals and trade-offs for all stakeholders.

A first methodological step for a sustainable product development could be the distinction between needs/demands and solutions pursued with QFD [13] which conforms to the ISO-standard 16355 for technology and product development process whereas user needs are defined as potential benefits employing a set of methods [14]. Requirements analysis with QFD may address sustainability of products within the time period of development.

For the deployment of sustainability on the long run, there are four different generic strategies pertinent in sustainability science, science-technology-studies and systemic design among others [15]:

1. **Efficiency:** focus on the preservation of environmental resources and avoid waste.

Sustainable digital product management should use personal, infrastructure and energy carefully. This is a matter of project and product management widening the scope of efficiency beyond costs. Contemporary sustainability accounting [16] provides an elaborate framework augmenting current control measures.

2. **Sufficiency:** focus on human needs ensuring that resources are dedicated to what is really needed.

Digital product management should focus on the fulfilment of relevant needs considering the priorities of different stakeholders form an operative and strategic level whereas trade-offs should be highly concerned as provided by the QFD toolkit of ISO 16355 [14]. If quality is defined not by specified requirements but as knowing why requirements cause good quality, product development should be more sustainable in terms of the comprehensive definition above serving as a measure for constructive quality assurance.

3. **Consistency:** focus on long-term usage and life-cycles of products.

The deeper the understanding of customer needs and the more flexible the development and delivery infrastructure for digital products, the longer should digital products survive. QFD should be elaborated thoroughly upstream for long term user needs and downstream for long term technical requirements for flexible digital infrastructures whereas trade-offs should be evaluated and considered properly.

4. **Resilience:** focus on the robustness to challenges.

Deep understanding and flexible infrastructures may contribute to resilience as well. However, agility of product development and management processes is of outmost importance in surviving unexpected challenges. 'Agile Software QFD' [17] could be employed for robust development of digital products and should be extended for a comprehensive agile digital product management approach.

There is a large body of knowledge on resource efficiency and agile development for resilience. This paper focusses on sufficiency and consistency where QFD and ISO 16355 promise new achievements beyond common research and practice of Digital Product Management. Starting from a theoretical discussion of sustainability for Digital Product Development and combining the knowledge on sustainability in general with the specific knowledge on Digital Product Management and related methodologies, this paper proceeds with the development of specific methodological framework for the deployment of sustainable Digital Product Management following the framework of design science for information systems research [18].

1.2   Strategic Goal Categories for Sustainable Digital Product Management

At the product level, needs are related to requirements. For strategic business planning, goals defining the business needs must be related to capabilities for its implementation which are typically projects. There is a common schema for strategic goals with the four categories: finance, customer, processes, learning and growth [19] (Fig. 1).

Fig. 1. Strategic Business Perspectives of the Classical Balanced Scorecard

This schema is called the 'balanced' scorecard, since enterprise is not achieved by financial performance only, it must be balanced with customer, process and learning/growth measures. Interactions are analysed explicitly in a strategy map. This conforms to the idea of the triple bottom line which does not explain how to balance it. It relates to the generic strategy of consistency in terms of the assurance of continuity and it may be balanced designing with a specific scorecard geared to the balance sustainability efforts considering the specific challenges of Digital Product Management.

Classical product development methodologies are driven primarily by technology neglecting the customer or user perspective. If software development is driven by the user, technology should be subordinate to the attainment of business goals unless it yields crucial performance for learning and growth. Furthermore, individual preferences of users may not be the best choice from a business perspective. Business process modelling pursues the improvement of structural organizational coordination which may reduce flexibility and autonomy of users. Technology, customer and business perspective are fundamental for the success of product management. The underlying conflicts conform to the discussion about resource-driven versus market-driven business strategy [19] and product-dominant and service-dominant logic in literature [21].

- Technology-driven methodology such the development of faster storage devices corresponds to resource-dominant logic;
- Customer-oriented methodology such as user experience design corresponds to service-dominant logic:

• Business-oriented methodology such as strategic information system planning or business process management corresponds to product-dominant logic.

Figure 2 depicts the three fundamental methodological paradigms and its interdependencies: Customer-driven design focuses the customer value and may fall short on technology and business value. Business process modelling pursues the improvement of the enterprises' structural organizational coordination but may reduce flexibility and autonomy of customers. Depending on the situation, different perspectives may be more important than the initial ones.

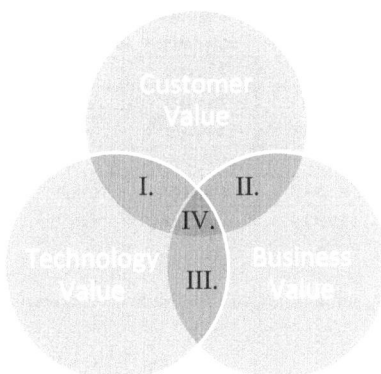

Fig. 2. Strategic Perspectives for Digital Product Management

In order to achieve sustainability in a strategic sense, the operationalisation of the perspectives must address long-term effects integrating the three perspectives hence considering trade-offs or potentials between.

  I. customer needs and technological requirements, such as usability versus security,
 II. customer needs and business goals, such as individualisation versus standardisation,
III. business goals and technological requirements, such as time-to-market versus maturity
IV. business goals, customer needs, and technological requirements e.g. regarding competition for shared resources

This schema classifies and helps to analyse shortcomings and establishes measures for the selection and design of software development methodology regarding sustainability from a strategic perspective. If a method omits a perspective or does not integrate perspectives, it may fall short in terms of methodological sustainability. As pointed out below, QFD appears to be suitable as a methodological framework for the deployment of comprehensive sustainable product development. This theoretical hypothesis will be evaluated by elaborating a specific QFD deployment in terms of design science research.

2   Methodological Evaluation

2.1   Sustainable Product Development with QFD

The majority of product development methodologies is dedicated to one perspective primarily. QFD is a quality management method which has been devised to capture the voice of the customer and to translate it into product requirements [14]. This relates to the methodological interface I in Fig. 2. The structure of a QFD matrix is depicted in Fig. 3.

		Product Requirement	Product Requirement	Product Requirement	...	Product Requirement
Customer Need	Priority	Impact	Impact	Impact	...	Impact
Customer Need	Priority	Impact	Impact	Impact	...	Impact
Customer Need	Priority	Impact	Impact	Impact	...	Impact
...	...	...	...	...	...	...
Customer Need	Priority	Impact	Impact	Impact	...	Impact
		Utility	Utility	Utility	...	Utility

Fig. 3. Schema of a QFD Matrix for a software product

After the elicitation of customer needs, product requirements, and prioritisation of customer needs by the user, the impact of each product requirement on each customer need is evaluated in a matrix, following the schema of Fig. 3 (the classical scale for the impacts is 0, 1, 3, 9). The scalar product of a specific requirement vector and the priority vector measure the total impact of the specific requirement on all customer needs (weighted by its priorities). This yields a measure for the 'utility' of each requirement. Requirements with low utility may be neglected, those with high utility are mandatory – a very important measure for product management decisions.

The employment of QFD for software development (Software QFD) has been established as a specific method for software requirements analysis [13] as well as and agile software development [17] among others. Within Software QFD, sustainability may appear in the customer needs (e.g. save energy) or as a product requirement (e.g. carbon footprint of the software system). Customer needs will rather express effectiveness whereas product requirements define the quality level and provide a lever for efficiency: the level should be balanced considering the impact on customer needs. If there is only a low impact, waste is to be avoided by decreasing the level. Hence the underlying rationale of the method QFD is directed towards sustainability which conforms to sustainability strategy type 2 – Sufficiency: only beneficial requirements will be implemented. If user needs do not change as fast as technology, e.g. for business standard software, it conforms to strategy type 3 – sufficiency as well: It is devised for long term usage.

2.2   Strategic Perspectives for Sustainable Product Management

With the emergence of ISO 16355 in 2015 [14], the scope of QFD has been extended from the specification of quality measures to the cross-departmental understanding of the reasons of good quality, which is far beyond the quality notion of common quality techniques. Thereby, the norm extends the scope of QFD beyond the customer and technology perspectives to the business perspective. Besides the voice of the customer and the analysis of product requirements, there is a voice of the business and an analysis of stakeholders and customer segments. But neither ISO 16355 nor any other literature provides a specific deployment or example for the integration of the business perspective for Digital Product Management (see Fig. 2). However, there are extensions of QFD called policy or strategy deployment some of them in conjunction with Hoshin Kanri [22]. Moreover, there are several concepts and cases on the application of QFD for strategic product planning and on QFD for IT product portfolio planning [23] but there is no concept for balancing the three methodological perspectives with regard to sustainability from a strategic perspective.

In order to address overall sustainability many levels of planning and many categories and interactions must be considered as elaborated above. The complexity of a comprehensive deployment would require many interrelated matrices which would not be a feasible starting point and a barrier for the adoption. Since digitalisation is inevitable for almost any business, it is moreover difficult to separate general business planning from IT planning and in the software business from software development. For a strategic product management approach, the different perspective must be clarified like in common balanced scorecard but geared to digital product management.

Internal versus External Resources

If natural or other resources are owned by the company sustainability is an obvious matter of business responsibility; if natural resources are public or exploited by external authorities which may not act responsible, it is a matter of societal responsibility or business ethics. It may but must not pay off in terms the corporate image or long-term business environment; it may be part of the corporate mission or a general business condition – an internal or an external factor. The differentiation of internal and external factors is an integral part of business strategy analysis (SWOT analysis, Porter's five forces etc.). Hence it is straightforward to differentiate the strategic analysis including sustainability by internal and external resources:

- *External resources*: Customers, suppliers, public authorities, nature, external research/knowledge …
- *Internal resources*: Financial, human, infrastructure (hardware/software), internal research/knowledge …

The lack or the decrease of an external resource is just as critical as that of an internal resource – however, it must be assessed and controlled differently. Hence internal and external resources establish two different planning perspectives and levels. Internal or external resources may not refer to the location, access or property necessarily. If a software product is distributed by a cloud by an external provider but access and control remain with the developer exclusively, it may be considered as an internal resource in terms of the application, but hardware and system software remain external. Finally, it is a strategic decision, whichever resources are considered internal or external. There are many enterprises which have limited control over the workforce due to several reasons, the (internal) workforce could be considered as an external resource factually.

Business Functions versus Temporary Activities

Doing business means transforming resources: utilising, maintaining, increasing and disposing them internally and externally. The transformation is structured in business functions geared to the business model – in the software business software development is a natural business function deploying external and/or internal resources. Whereas internal and external resources are either product or outcome-related form of sustainability, the performance of the business function is process-related. In a process-oriented organisation, business functions are represented by business processes comprising the essential business activities operating the business model and – if designed well – they are supposed to ensure lasting business success. However, there are cross-functional activities which are non-routine and are often organised in a complementary process organisation which requires a different approach for planning and control. Whereas a business function is deployed permanently and is supposed to generate lasting value, projects or other actions are temporarily, contribute to the value of resources or support business functions regarding value creation. They should not exist for a long time and then cease to exist. Hence, temporary or non-routine activities such as projects and other actions require a separate planning perspective.

Strategic Perspectives for Sustainable Product Deployment

Resources as the static elements as well as permanent and temporary activities as dynamic elements build the four perspectives of strategic sustainability deployment in Fig. 4 as a basis for a balanced scorecard for strategic sustainability deployment.

Business functions and temporary activities (projects etc.) transform external and internal resources. Internal resources represent capabilities such as technology leadership (resource-based view) whereas a high service level is an internal process resource which is supposed to improve customer satisfaction, which are external resources. Sustainable customer satisfaction requires sustainable service levels and technological capabilities among others.

Fig. 4. Four strategic perspectives for sustainable product deployment

What is the right service level? Is it feasible to improve customer satisfaction if a high level has already been achieved? How much efforts and money should be invested into product innovation and how much in the maintenance of the installed base? In order to answer all of these questions, resources and activities must be balanced wisely over time.

2.3 Sustainable Strategy Deployment with QFD

Starting with the QFD matrix for interface I (see Fig. 3) balancing customer and technology value, ISO 16355 proposes the analysis of the voice of the customer for each QFD project. From a strategic perspective, one single QFD matrix for one application is just a single project. The impact of the project as a whole is to be determined, not the impact of some requirements on some customer needs (Fig. 5).

		Project	Project	Project	Project	Project
Business Goal	Priority	Impact	Impact	Impact	...	Impact
Business Goal	Priority	Impact	Impact	Impact	...	Impact
Business Goal	Priority	Impact	Impact	Impact	...	Impact
...	...	...	...	...	...	...
Business Goal	Priority	Impact	Impact	Impact	...	Impact
		Utility	Utility	Utility	...	Utility

Fig. 5. Schema of a QFD matrix for the prioritisation of projects

The utility of projects measures the potential contribution to business goal or goal alignment but does not support the balancing of goals by its structure automatically. If business goals include customer-related and technology-related goals, interface II and III could be addressed. If business goals are augmented by environmental or social sustainability, overall balancing could be achieved at the project planning level: economic goals and environmental goals are balanced by prioritisation. For consulting companies, projects are the primary planning entity but not for software houses and other IT service providers maintaining an installed base. Following the schema in Fig. 4 a second QFD matrix should be set up for the prioritisation of business functions as depicted in Fig. 6.

		Business Function	Business Function	Business Function	...	Business Function
Business Goal	Priority	Impact	Impact	Impact	...	Impact
Business Goal	Priority	Impact	Impact	Impact	...	Impact
Business Goal	Priority	Impact	Impact	Impact	...	Impact
...	...	...	...	...	...	...
Business Goal	Priority	Impact	Impact	Impact	...	Impact
		Utility	Utility	Utility	...	Utility

Fig. 6. Schema of a QFD Matrix for the prioritisation of Business Functions

According to Fig. 4, there are at least four planning entities and four interfaces for top-down planning:

- Multi-perspective definition and prioritisation of business goals concerning external resources
- Definition of business functions and evaluation of its utility regarding external resources
- Definition of projects and evaluation of its utility regarding external resources
- Multi-perspective definition of business goals concerning internal resources and evaluation of the impact of business functions and projects on internal resources.

Top-down planning means, that the business is geared to external forces following a market-based approach or other, depending on the relevance of external resources. In a capability-based approach, the planning would be bottom-up, starting with the internal resources yielding the impact on external resources. Whichever approach is appropriate or desired depends on the business environment, mission/vision, stakeholders etc. All in all, the schema is flexible and could be tailored to suit any specific situation. However, it is recommended to start the schema/concept with two entities first – project prioritisation is in most cases a good choice – and to extend it step by step. It is not an engineering process but an evolution.

2.4 Sample Strategic Sustainability Deployment with QFD

An advanced deployment schema requires several steps and interrelated matrices. A simplified example is depicted in Fig. 7. It comprises a set of four interrelated matrices in a setup like an X – called X-Matrix [14].

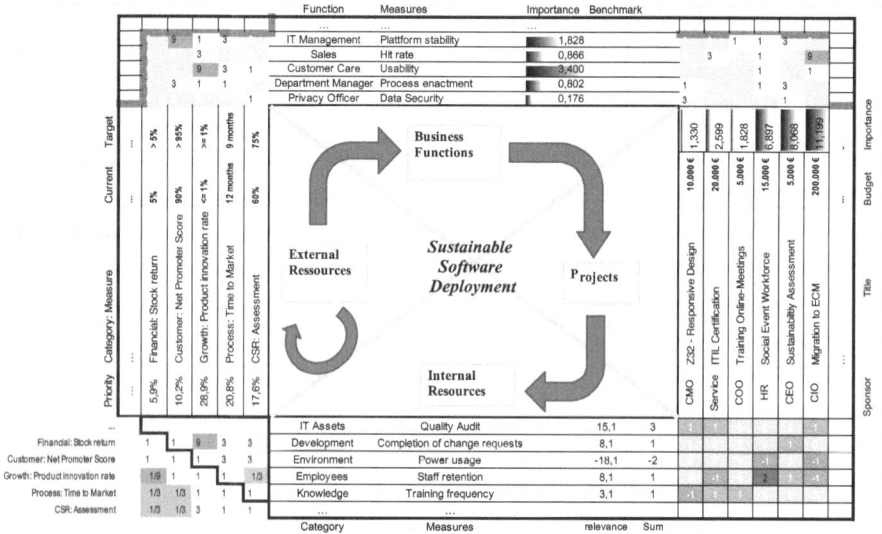

Fig. 7. Example of strategic sustainability deployment

External resources are defined on the left side following the categories of the balanced scorecard extended by CSR (category: goal). Prioritisation is conducted with pairwise comparison according to AHP [14] in the left lower corner yielding the priority in the row above. Business functions are specified in the top middle rows, whereas several functions are related to software development, but there are no such business functions. Software development is organised in cross-functional projects. The impact of business functions on external resources is evaluated in the left upper corner (compare to Fig. 3). The sum of the impacts weighted by its priorities measures the importance or value for the attainment of the business goals regarding external resources. Customer care has the highest impact but far, hence it deserves special attention and is access to scarce resources. The impact of data security has been evaluated as quite low – the evaluation may reproduce management bias.

Projects are specified on the right side. They are initiated by a sponsor responsible for the allocation of budget: CMO, service department, etc. Projects are prioritised in the upper right corner (compare to Fig. 3). The highest utility has the migration to ECM, it is of outmost importance for the external resources, sustainability assessment is secondary. Adequacy of budget, personal, infrastructure etc. should be checked and balanced eventually. Finally, internal resources are considered in the bottom column, such as IT assets, software development capabilities and power usage. For each internal resource a measure is provided as a benchmark for the assessment of the impact of the projects which is conducted in the right lower corner employing a Pugh matrix [13] indicating positive and negative effects which are summed up and weighted by the importance of the project in order to evaluate the relevance of the impact. Power usage appears to be a crucial issue, which would have not been raised from the external perspective and without considering different types of sustainability.

2.5   Sample Analysis of Trade-Offs Between Sustainability Goals with QFD

The QFD deployments presented above do not address the analysis of trade-offs between goals/needs and/or requirements. The analysis of interactions is an integral feature of the classical "House of Quality": interactions between quality elements are elaborated in a triangular half-matrix assuming that interactions are symmetric (independent of its direction) and depicted as the 'roof' of the QFD-matrix [24]. ISO 16355 does not explain the 'roof' or provide examples for its setup and interpretation. There is no pertinent description of it in the literature. The author has carried out an internal evaluation of research projects on sustainability with the result that the trade-offs between the sustainability goals tend to be symmetrical. Sustainability effect are not well-defined mechanical effects but more complex.

Figure 8 depicts a cross-impact matrix of strategic sustainability goals regarding a specific research scenario employing the QFD-scales for the metrication of impact. The seventeen sustainability goals of the United Nations [25] build the matrix of trade-offs by columns and rows.

The matrix is sparse and most trade-offs are positive (green). It is quite large and bulky to handle. This suggest that not all aspects are relevant and the matrix should be skimmed. Several measures such as active/passive sum or the activity level are calculated in order to draw conclusions concerning sustainability matters, though it is difficult to

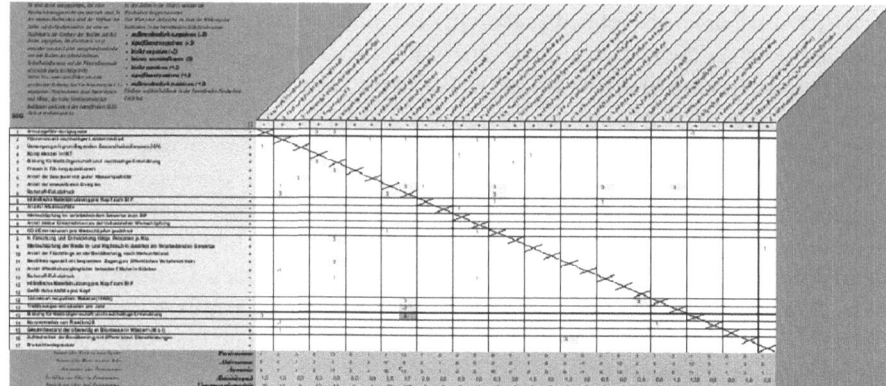

Fig. 8. Analysis of trade-offs between the sustainability development goals of the UN (Color figure online)

interpret. Hence, further research is required for the setup and assessment of the impact of interactions on the attainment of goals or the utility of requirements, which is – if employed for the evaluation of measures for sustainability – quite significant for product management.

3 Conclusion and Outlook

Balancing development methodology in general and digital product management specifically: the structure is similar; the criteria are different. However, it requires a flexible, multi-perspective approach and an augmentation and tailoring of criteria and instruments. Strategic QFD suits this challenge well and may be scaled from a simple prioritisation matrix to multi-stage deployment. Further research is required to validate the approach in different application scenarios and branches.

Acknowledgments. Part of this research has been funded by Aachen University of Applied Sciences. The author would like to express his gratitude for the constructive feedback of the reviewers which helped to improve the paper significantly.

References

1. Loeser, F.: Green IT and green IS: definition of constructs and overview of current practices. In: 19th Americas Conference on Information Systems, Chicago, IL, pp. 936–952 (2013)
2. Groher, I., Weinreich, R.: An interview study on sustainability concerns in software development projects. In: 43rd Euromicro Conference on Software Engineering and Advanced Applications (SEAA), Vienna, Austria, pp. 350–358 (2017)
3. Donaldson, S.E.; Siegel, S.G.: Successful Software Development, 2nd edn. Prentice Hall PTR, Upper Saddle River, NJ (2001)
4. Schmidt, B., Wytzisk, A.: Nachhaltigkeitsaspekte in der Softwareentwicklung. In: Englert, M.; Ternès, A. (eds.) Nachhaltiges Management, pp. 651–668. Springer Gabler, Heidelberg (2019). https://doi.org/10.1007/978-3-662-57693-9_34

5. Böttcher, T.P., Empelmann, S., Weking, J., Hein, A., Krcmar, H.: Digital sustainable business models: using digital technology to integrate ecological sustainability into the core of business models. Inf. Syst. J. **34**(3), 736–761 (2024)
6. Sousa-Zomer, T.T., Miguel, P.A.C.: A QFD-based approach to support sustainable product-service systems conceptual design. Int. J. Adv. Manuf. Technol. **88**, 701–717 (2017)
7. Dhiman, S.: Product, people, and planet: the triple bottom line sustainability imperative. J. Glob. Bus. Issues **2**(2), 51–57 (2008)
8. Alhaddi, H.: Triple bottom play and sustainability: a literature review. Bus. Manag. Stud. **2**(1), 6–10 (2015)
9. Kotlarsky, J., Oshri, I., Sekulic, N.: Digital sustainability in information systems research: conceptual foundations and future directions. J. Assoc. Inf. Syst. **24**(4), 936–952 (2023)
10. Norman, W., MacDonald, C.: Getting to the bottom of "triple bottom line." Bus. Ethics Q. **14**(2), 243–262 (2004)
11. Moore, J.E., Mascarenhas, A., Bain, J., Straus, S.E.: Developing a comprehensive definition of sustainability. Implementation Sci. **12**(110) (2017). https://rdcu.be/dKhUT
12. IEEE Standard Glossary of Software Engineering Terminology, 610.12-1990, p. 62. IEEE (2002)
13. Herzwurm, G., Schockert, S., Pietsch, W.: QFD for customer-focused requirements engineering. In: Proceedings of the 11th IEEE International Requirements Engineering Conference, Monterey Bay, USA, pp. 330–338 (2003)
14. ISO 16355-1:2015: Applications of statistical and related methods to new technology and product development process - Part 1: General principles and perspectives of Quality Function Deployment (QFD), International Standards Organization, Geneva, Switzerland (2015)
15. Hediger, W.: Reconciling "weak" and "strong" sustainability. Int. J. Soc. Econ. **26**(7/8/9), 1120–1144 (1999)
16. Schaltegger, S., Christ, K.L., Wenzig, J., Burritt, R.L.: Corporate sustainability management accounting and multi-level links for sustainability–a systematic review. Int. J. Manag. Rev. **24**(4), 480–500 (2022)
17. Schockert, S.: Agiles Software Quality Function Deployment, Eul, Siegburg (2017)
18. Hevner, A.R., March, S.T., Park, J., Ram, S.: Design science in information systems design. MIS Q. **28**(1), 75–105 (2004)
19. Kaplan, R.S., Norton, D.P.: The Strategy-Focused Organization: How Balanced Scorecard Companies Thrive in the New Business Environment. Boston, MA, 1 October 2000
20. Barney, J.B.: Is the resource-based 'view' a useful perspective for strategic management research? Acad. Manag. Rev. **26**(1), 101 (2001)
21. Vargo, S.L., Lusch, R.F.: Evolving to a new dominant logic for marketing. J. Mark. **68**(1), 1–17 (2004)
22. Ennals, R.: Hoshin Kanri: the strategic approach to continuous improvement. AI Soc. **25**(3), 371–372 (2010)
23. Pietsch, W.: Effective management of interrelated IT projects – employing policy deployment for IT governance. In: Proceeding of the 11th International Symposium on QFD in Kusadasi, QFD-Institute, Michigan (2005)
24. Ficalora, J.P., Cohen, L.: Quality Function Deployment and Six SIGMA – A QFD Handbook. Prentice Hall (2012)
25. United Nations: The Sustainable Development Goals, in Achieving our own humanity, pp. 142–147, United Nations (2020)

Understanding DevOps Critical Success Factors: A Thematic Analysis

Nasreen Azad$^{(\boxtimes)}$, Sami Hyrynsalmi, and Kari Smolander

LUT University, Lappeenranta, Finland
{nasren.azad,sami.hyrynsalmi,kari.smolander}@lut.fi

Abstract. The software development industry has widely adopted DevOps culture and practices, which emphasize the importance of effective utilization of DevOps tools, promoting collaboration, developing necessary skills among employees, and fostering a supportive company culture. Understanding the critical success factors for DevOps is essential for ensuring the overall performance of an organization. To gain a deeper understanding of DevOps practices and insights from professionals during the adoption of DevOps within teams, a study was conducted aimed at identifying DevOps critical success factors for teams within software-producing organizations. The study employed a thematic approach through collaborative coding and extensive interviews with 16 DevOps professionals in the IT industry. The findings highlighted the importance of fostering a (1) collaborative organizational culture, (2) Integrating DevOps automation, (3) cultivating strong work ethics, (4) addressing challenges related to remote teamwork, and (5) establishing dedicated DevOps security teams. Our findings thus contribute to improving DevOps concepts of success factors, practices, and organizational impacts.

Keywords: DevOps · Critical Success Factors · Software Development · Software Operations · Thematic analysis · Qualitative research

1 Introduction

As technology evolves, the software development industry must rapidly adapt to emerging trends to remain competitive and relevant in the market [39]. Prioritizing product quality, efficient testing, timely releases, and swift time-to-market are crucial for success in this dynamic landscape [25].

The adoption of DevOps has surged in recent years, with substantial investments from IT organizations and software industries [19]. The global DevOps market is projected to experience robust growth, indicating its increasing importance [19]. However, successful DevOps adoption impacts significant cultural and organizational shifts within IT departments [8,35]. The research conducted by Shahin et al. [41] identified seven critical success factors (CSFs) essential for continuous practices, including testing, transparency, team awareness, design principles, customer environment, a motivated and highly skilled team, accurate infrastructure, and application domain. However, these factors lack explicit validation. Dikert et al. [20] highlighted the need for additional research to identify

D. Petrik et al. (Eds.): ICDPM 2024, LNBIP 528, pp. 28–43, 2025.
https://doi.org/10.1007/978-3-031-71515-0_3

challenges and determine the most significant success factors for agile transformations, emphasizing the importance of discerning genuine critical relevance for organizations [8].

Scholars have explored the impact of CSFs on organizational performance, emphasizing the intricate relationship between successful implementation and organizational improvement [4,6,8,40]. Linking organizational success to identified CSFs is crucial for effective measurement, encompassing tangible benefits like cost reduction and intangible benefits such as customer satisfaction and project success [8,9].

The implementation and adoption of DevOps has witnessed significant growth in recent years in terms of investment for IT organizations and software industries, with most surveys indicating a notable surge in DevOps adoption [19]. According to the DevOps Trends Survey study 2023, the global DevOps market is projected to experience a robust compound annual growth rate of approximately 20 to 25 percent until 2030 [19]. Despite this upward trend, achieving successful DevOps adoption remains contingent on profound cultural and organizational shifts within companies' IT departments. However, organizations often face challenges when formulating a DevOps adoption strategy and establishing effective team structures. This difficulty in defining a coherent strategy and structuring teams successfully can adversely affect team performance and success [8,15].

Despite increasing interest and academic inquiry into DevOps, a comprehensive understanding of critical success factors for its effective implementation remains elusive [4,5,7,23]. In response to this research gap, we have applied thematic analysis based on 16 professional interviews to understand various success factors and their relationship with DevOps practices. To address the aim of this research we have one research question (RQ).

RQ: What is the significance of Critical Success Factors (CSF) in DevOps practices within IT organizations?

This research paper makes three key contributions. Firstly, it enhances understanding of DevOps success factors by synthesizing existing literature and interview data. Secondly, it offers detailed insights into DevOps implementation and its impact on organizational performance. Lastly, it provides practical recommendations for organizations to improve their DevOps practices, bridging theory with actionable guidance for practitioners.

The remaining of the study is structured as follows. Section 2 presents the empirical research strategy, followed by results in Sect. 3. Section 4 summarizes the essential findings, Sect. 4 presents the discussion, Sect. 5 explains related work, and Sect. 6 presents the study's conclusion.

2   Research Process

2.1   Data Collection

We conducted semi-structured interviews, c.f. [26], with 16 DevOps professionals from the software development industry actively engaged in DevOps practices.

Each interview session lasted approximately 45 min, during which we obtained permission from the participants to record the discussions. In total, we dedicated 12 h to conducting these interviews, during which the respondents generously shared valuable insights drawn from their current and past experiences in DevOps. The extensive discussions yielded substantial data, resulting in 480 pages of transcribed documents for subsequent analysis. The interviews were conducted in the second quarter of 2022 and involved professionals from five countries: Finland, Sweden, Norway, Germany, and the United Kingdom. We employed various recruitment methods to ensure a diverse pool of participants, specifically those working in DevOps. Initially, we leveraged personal contacts and professional networks on social media platforms such as Twitter and LinkedIn to identify potential candidates. Subsequently, we reached out to them via email and private messages to gauge their interest in participating in our study and sharing their insights.

Furthermore, we utilized the snowball recruitment technique to expand our participant pool [46,47]. This method allowed us to identify additional professionals through referrals from initial interviewees, thereby enriching the diversity of perspectives in our research. The interviews were scheduled based on the availability of the participants. They were conducted in teams using a predefined set of guiding questions that covered our research's main areas of interest [45] (Table 1).

2.2 Data Extraction and Analysis

Data was first coded based on interviews, and later on, the data synthesis was done [29]. The analysis process was initiated using a thematic coding technique outlined by Braun and Clarke [16,17]. The researchers extracted success factors and professionals' perspectives regarding DevOps practices from the interview quotes and applied them to the analysis. Firstly, the researchers aimed to identify critical success factors for DevOps practices. Secondly, they tried to understand professionals' perspectives on DevOps practices according to success factors. Thirdly, they tried to find connections between DevOps' success factors and organizational practices. The researchers developed a set of predefined themes from the transcripts. They analyzed and discussed the results and followed a strict process to resolve disagreements. The researchers familiarized themselves with the data collection, engaged in-depth discussions based on the interviews, and went through a rigorous process to analyze the data.

We started gathering data from the professional's mentions of success factors and organizational practices in the transcriptions. For Example, *"Initially, we relied on GitHub and Jenkins as our primary tools. However, DevOps represents a cultural shift in product and service companies' operations. In the DevOps approach, developers are more actively engaged with customers and have greater exposure to real customer problems. For me, the essence of DevOps lies in automation and the effective use of tools"*- (R8) is an example of how good tooling helps developers to perform better for customers' needs through automation. Similarly, the quote, *"Currently, in most applications, this is infrastructure as code because nowadays, everything goes into the cloud. We are no longer using*

Table 1. Participant's Demographic information and working practices, SN represents Respondents from R1–R16, Respondents' role in the company, Domain, Team location, Team types, Team members in the team, Countries, and Number of employees

ID	Role in Com	Domain	Team location	Team types	Team members	Country	No of employees in the comp.	Tools	Sw.dev. method	Exp in SWD (yr)
R1	Cloud Engineer	IT	Co-located	Developers	14	Finland	571(s)	Docker GitLab Scrum		10
R2	Cloud Engineer	Energy company	Co-located	Developers	10	Finland	19000 (L)	GitLab Kubernetes	N/A	3
R3	Site Reliability Engineer	Semiconductor and Software company	Co-located	Developers	20	UK	6210(M)	Docker Azure CI/CD	Kanban	8
R4	DevOps consultant	DevOps consulting company	Distributed	Developers	8	Germany	not mentioned	GitLab, Docker, Ansible	Scrum, CI/CD,	10
R5	DevOps Engineer	Digital Branding company	Co-located	Full stack developer	10	Norway	6000(M)	GitLab, Azure, Terraform	Kanban, Scrum	4.5
R6	Software Developer	Financial Consultant	Co-located	Front-end and back-end Developers	10	Finland	24(S) JIRA CI /CD GitHub	Circle CI		7
R7	Technical PM	Global cyber security	Co-located	Developers	15	Finland	16566(s)	GitHub Docker Jira Kanban	Scrum	9
R8	CTO	Digital Wallets	Distributed	DevOps Engineers	7	Sweden	15(S)	GitHub, Azure, Aws	scrum, Kanban	16
R9	Tech lead	DevOps company	Co-locate	DevOps engineers	8	Finland	38(S)	JIRA, Terraform, Azure	Kanban	10
R10	DevOps Engineer	Business	co-located	Developer	10	Germany	4238(M)	Docker Terraform JIRA	Scrum	7
R11	Cloud Engineer	DevOps company	Co-located	Full stack developer	7	Finland	1389(S)	Docker Bamboo Docker	Kanban	8
R12	CTO	IT Security	co-located	DevOps Engineer	13	Finland	590(S)	GitHub AWS Terraform	Kanban	5
R13	Jr. software developer	Insurance company	Distributed	DevOps Engineer	8	Sweden	1400(S)	GitLab Kibana Jenkins Terraform	scrum	6
R14	DevOps Engineer	IT company	Co-located	DevSecods engineer	10	Sweden	2000(M)	Ansible Bamboo Docker	scrum	9
R15	Senior software developer	DevOps company	Distributed	DevOps Engineer	8	Norway	278(S)	Jenkins Jira Gitlab	Kanban	6
R16	DevOps Engineer	IT Consulting company	Distributed	DevOps Engineer	6	UK	943(S)	GitHub Docker Kubernetes Ansible	Kanban	10

one-premise data centers. So, our main goal is to clarify everything. If we want to deploy everything into the cloud, it gets messy. It's also time-consuming, and we want to automate things. so, we use infrastructure as a code which speeds up the automation process."-(R2) denotes a professional's recommendation where using infrastructure as code for DevOps makes the automation process work faster and more efficiently.

We tried to group two similar mentions equally regarding the main idea shared in the interviews. So, we analyzed those two similar mentions as one idea. Here are example quotes from the analysis:

"Well, there is always room for improvement. I think the main thing is to understand development operations and security. We want to include or if you want to talk about like DevSecOps or DevOps. So, we need to understand each other's perspective"-(R2). *"There are always challenges in the software development process. If we integrate security from the beginning, it would be better for the process. So, I saw that people don't understand the importance of security. The whole thing should be conducted because it's not only just developing, it's also like securing the applications for the long run"*-(R8).

In the above example, both quotes refer to the importance of implementing security from the start of the development process. We use the thematic analysis framework proposed by Braun and Clarke [16] to create themes that summarize the data. During the familiarization phase, the researchers take the necessary steps to become familiar with the data. To do this, researchers review the transcriptions thoroughly.

We meticulously analyzed the data we collected. We assigned unique codes to the data entries, briefly describing the interviewees' words. These codes were used to categorize and organize the data for analysis. To ensure a fair and accurate analysis, the researchers divided the work into three parts, allowing each author to focus on specific aspects of the data. Each author followed a detailed procedure outlined at the beginning of the subsection to ensure consistency in the analysis process. This methodical approach allowed the researchers to analyze the data and draw meaningful conclusions.

The researchers start to sort the codes into themes. Some themes might be sub-themes of others, or some codes can become themes if they are pertinent. In Fig. 1, we show how codes, themes, and categories are connected and emerge from the data. In Fig. 1, we give an example of the coding process. In the figure, there are 3 example themes *"Development culture and mindset"*, *"DevOps working Ethics"*, and *"Tools for supporting DevOps"*. In the coding phase of *"Development culture and mindset"*, there are four codes named *"Having a collaboration in teams"*, *"Distributing the responsibilities"*, *"Knowledge sharing in teams"*, and *"DevOps perception"*. In the *"Ethical issues for DevOps"* theme has five codes naming *"Leadership issues in teams"*, *"Toxic culture in workplace"*, *"Discrimination in teams"*, *"Unrealistic goals"* and *"Unethical use of company tools"*. In the third theme of *"Tools for supporting DevOps"*, there are four codes naming *"Continuous integration"*, *"Automation"*, *"Continuous monitoring"*, *"Continu-*

ous testing and delivery". All three categories are connected to the concept of implementation of DevOps practices.

A discrepancy between different success factors, professional recommendations, and organizational performance can be attributed to an inconsistency. This inconsistency can occur because the challenges and recommendations reflect the specific DevOps practices being used, which may be different from the experiences of others.

3   Results and Findings

3.1   Themes

Collaboration and DevOps Culture. Every organization has a team culture that differs from one organization to another. DevOps culture aims to create collaboration between the developers and Ops people [2,4,6–9]. During our interviews; we got much insightful information about DevOps culture in organizations and how in practice it works for both teams. This collaboration culture impacts CSF and company performance. One respondent quoted that,

"There are several very experienced team members. Due to that, sometimes there is not much knowledge gap there, but we have resource gap like we need more people"- R1 (Cloud Engineer, Finland).

A professional from an IT company stated that *"Being like in culture, where everyone contributes and everyone kind of understands each other's point of view. We want to break this wall or silos so that we make the software development process faster"* - R2 (Cloud Engineer, Finland)

DevOps and Working Ethics. Ethical issues in software development are very crucial in terms of organizational, social, and technical contexts [5]. Ethics has a role in organizations' performance which also connects critical success factors to some extent [5]. Software developers should consider ethics while working on the software development lifecycle [10,43]. When there is an unethical software issue it is followed by many consequences depending on who the users or audience of the software usage [43].

According to a professional *"To handle work ethics when working in a team, it's best to have a small, integrated team where everyone is engaged in the development process from start to finish. This enables developers and teams to facilitate ethical conversations and eliminate toxic culture and poor leadership."* - R15 (Senior Software Developer, Norway).

DevOps Automation. DevOps automation is a practice or discipline of using different software tools and methodologies to automate some repetitive and manual tasks to make the software process faster [3,11]. By adopting automation, a company can reduce risks and streamline the process. Some teams can adopt the automation process and get an advantage while testing codes to make the deployment [4,9]. Some companies partially use automation for specific tasks. For better software performance teams should automate most of the processes [13].

Table 2. The propositions identified in this study.

ID	Identified proposition
P1	Team collaboration facilitates the Development culture and mindset of teams
P2	Responsibility distribution facilitates the Development culture and mindset of teams
P3	Knowledge sharing facilitates the Development culture and mindset of teams
P4	DevOps perception might facilitate the Development culture and mindset of teams
P5	Leadership issues in teams decrease teams' ethical working environment
P6	Toxic culture in the workplace decreases ethical working environment in teams
P7	Discrimination in teams decrease ethical working environment in teams
P8	Unethical use of tools decreases ethical working environment in teams
P9	Continuous integration increases DevOps implementation practices
P10	Automation increases DevOps implementation practices
P11	Continuous monitoring increases DevOps implementation practices
P12	DevOps implementation practices support quality assurance for the product
P13	DevOps implementation practices support continuous measurement for DevOps teams
P14	DevOps implementation practices support collaborative culture for the teams
P15	DevOps implementation practices are enhanced with DevOps security
P16	Remote work negatively decreases DevOps implementation practices

According to a developer *"Because it is possible that you just push the code, someone will review the code and after that, you don't have to do anything. If there is 100 percent automation, You just wait and it should be in production after the auto-continuous testing and continuous integration. All of these tasks will be done automatically, So the developer has fewer things to handle"* - R1 (Cloud Engineer, Finland)

Remote Teamwork Challenge. Software engineering is a highly technical, knowledge-oriented task that combines collaboration and coordination with developers and stakeholders. This task also requires a very focused and uninterrupted work process from developers' commitment so that they can efficiently develop good quality and efficient software for the software industry [37]. Very often software is developed by open-source communities, remotely, and distributed software projects are globally distributed [22].

A tech lead mentioned that *"Remote work requires tools for developers to produce code, build and deploy software from anywhere. Embedded tools help teams communicate and perform efficiently, eliminating poor communication and time zone challenges"* - R9 (Tech Lead, Finland).

DevOps Security Teams. DevSecOps is a security testing integration practice that is involved in every stage of the software development process [38]. This encourages collaboration between developers, security specialists, and operations teams so that the software is built efficiently and secured for the system with the help of tools and processes [38]. DevSecOps helps in the cultural transformation which makes security a shared responsibility for those who are involved in building the software. In DevSevOps, security takes place earlier in the development cycle, and it is already in the planning phase before the deployment is done for production [49].

IT professionals stated that *"The importance of DevSecOps in the development process is crucial. There are some advantages to having a security check earlier. It reduces human errors by automating security testing. Thus, the security assessment prevents the bottleneck situation in the development process"*-R7 (Technical Project Manager, Finland).

3.2   Towards a Theory for DevOps CSF

This section summarizes the CSF theory with the recommendations and reporting from software engineering disciplines [42]. While describing a theory, it should have constructs, propositions, scope, and explanations [36]. Here, we propose a sample of CSF theory that influences different organizational issues. DevOps critical success factors are the central concept that helps build a company culture between development and operation teams. DevOps CSF is supported by other concepts, including Development culture and mindset. In Fig. 1, the first box on the left represents Development culture and mindset. For example, Collaboration in teams, responsibility distribution, Knowledge sharing, and DevOps perception represent the concept of development culture and mindset. The second box on the left represents Ethical issues for DevOps meaning Leadership issues, Toxic culture in the workplace, discrimination in teams, unethical use of tools, etc.). The last box on the left represents the concept of tools for supporting DevOps, which means continuous integration, automation, and monitoring. On the right side in Fig. 1 assuring quality, continuous measure, collaboration culture, DevOps security teams, and remote teamwork impacts on DevOps organizational performances. Based on categories and concepts, relationships of subcategories, and transcription memos we have identified 16 propositions. In Fig. 2 the proposed propositions and relationships are shown.

In Fig. 2 the theory elements are represented and the relationships between development teams and operation teams are highlighted. According to our findings, DevOps implementation practices support quality assurance (P12), Continuous measure (P13), and collaboration culture (P14) in IT organizations. DevOps security (P15) is good for DevOps implementation practices and is enhanced with DevOps security. A good security team's involvement from the beginning of the process gives more secure applications for the users. For the proposition of remote work (P16), we have found that Remote work decreases DevOps implementation practices, and the engineers suggested that remote work decreases confidence and communication problems and improves the development process. Team collaboration (P1), responsibility distribution (P2), knowledge sharing (P3), and DevOps perception(P4) might facilitate the Development culture and mindset of teams. We have also found that leadership issues (P5), toxic culture (P6), discrimination in teams (P7), and unethical use of tools (P8) in teams decrease teams' ethical working environment, and that makes the project fail. Continuous integration (P9), automation (P10) and continuous monitoring (P11) increase DevOps implementation practices in teams.

4   Discussion

4.1   Key Findings

Insights into Critical Success Factors can significantly impact DevOps practices in IT organizations by providing a framework for understanding and prioritizing key elements that contribute to the success of DevOps initiatives [6]. By identifying and focusing on factors critical to success, organizations can ensure that DevOps initiatives are in sync with overall business objectives [4,8]. This ensures that key factors contributing to success receive the necessary attention and resources, which increases the likelihood of successful DevOps adoption, improves collaboration, and delivers high-quality software with greater efficiency [4,7,8].

Insights into CSFs provide a basis for continuous improvement. Regularly assessing and refining the critical success factors allows organizations to adapt and evolve their DevOps practices to meet changing business needs and technological advancements. Understanding CSFs related to cultural aspects leads to initiatives that promote a DevOps-friendly work environment, which is crucial for fostering a collaborative and innovative culture [1,3,4,7,8,12,13]. CSFs may highlight the importance of automation and effective tooling, which organizations should leverage insights to invest in the right tools and technologies that align with DevOps principles, enhancing efficiency and reducing manual interventions in the software delivery pipeline. CSFs often involve defining relevant metrics for measuring the success of DevOps practices. Insights into these metrics enable organizations to monitor performance, identify bottlenecks, and continuously optimize their processes [4–9].

4.2   Implications for Academia

Academic researchers play a pivotal role in conducting interdisciplinary research in DevOps, as their work is crucial for the evolution of this field [32]. However, there is a need for more research due to the education system's adaptability to evolving market demands [32]. Enhancing industrial and market relevance skills and emphasizing efficient work methodologies, such as automation tasks and agile and DevOps practices, are essential knowledge to learn. Knowing empirical research on the impact of DevOps on organizational performance and the challenges during implementation is critical [14]. Updating curricula to include DevOps practices ensures students are equipped with industry-aligned skills. Researchers must conduct various research, including agile methodologies and dynamics, and study DevOps practices. Additionally, exploring the impact of automation and efficient collaboration on productivity is crucial [14].

4.3 Implications for Practice

Professionals' perspectives can be applied to DevOps practices to generate insights and strategies that are directly applicable to real-world contexts. In Table 2, we have outlined the practical guidelines recommended by industry professionals for optimizing the performance of Development and Operations practices within DevOps teams (Table 3).

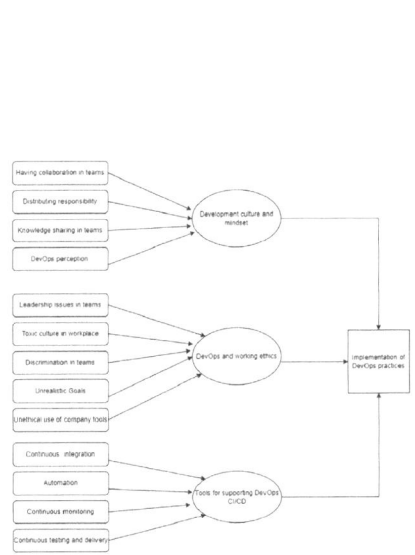

Fig. 1. Coding process for DevOps Implementation practices

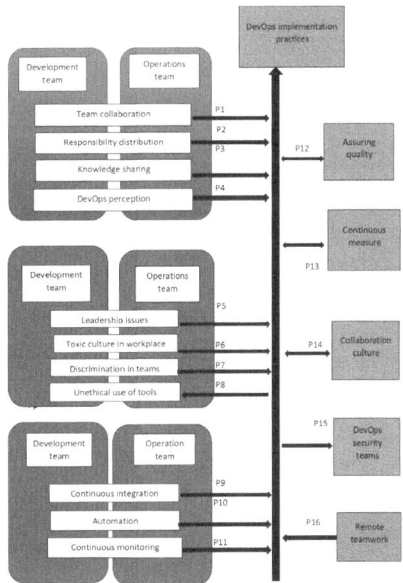

Fig. 2. Theory for DevOps critical success factors

5 Related Work

5.1 DevOps Practices and Success Factors

Customers now have higher demands and expectations, and they expect software applications to be of higher quality and delivered in a quicker time [4]. Many different methods are utilized by companies for software development, with agile practices being one of the most widely used. However, the issue with agile practices is that they tend to only cater to the development side, leaving out the operations team. In order to have a complete software process, it is necessary to have both the development and operations teams working together [27]. In order for a software development project to generate business value, it is imperative that the software be deployed to the production environment. Without

Table 3. Practical guidelines for DevOps teams

Practical guidelines	Recommendations for teams
Facilitate the exchange of knowledge and promote collaborative learning.	To optimize the team's knowledge and support system, we highly recommend implementing standards for knowledge sharing and learning opportunities among team members. This involves adapting the necessary knowledge for plan, building, and run activities associated with specific products.
Collaborate and coordinate with teams from different departments to achieve common goals.	One effective strategy is to combine teams from different departments to take full responsibility for the entire delivery process of one or more IT products. To ensure strong teamwork and accountability, it is recommended that the team's approach be product-focused rather than project-focused. This approach will help to create a sense of coherence and social responsibility within the team.
Teams must take swift action to address toxic cultures and discrimination and ethical concerns.	The team's working culture should be professional, friendly, and free from discrimination and unethical behavior as it has a significant impact on team productivity.
Teams must enable the identification of critical success factors specific to the DevOps implementation within a given organization.	Organizations can focus their efforts on factors empirically linked to success, potentially accelerating the adoption and integration of DevOps practices.
Teams should customize training and skills development.	Training programs and skill development initiatives can be customized to address the specific needs identified within team practices by ensuring a more targeted and effective approach to process development
Continuous improvement based on real-world experiences.	Organizations can adapt their DevOps practices in real-time, responding to changing needs and circumstances with insights derived from an ongoing practical approaches.

such deployment, even if the software development process was completed in an expeditious manner, the project will fail to yield any tangible benefits for the business. It is, therefore, crucial for organizations to ensure that their software development efforts culminate in the successful deployment of the software to production [6,7,27].

DevOps practices can improve software performance, collaboration, integration, and communication [4,7,11]. There is no specific definition for DevOps, though many concepts surround it [28]. The purpose of DevOps is to bridge the gap between teams and enable efficient software development [51]. DevOps merges development and operations teams and aims to deliver software features faster to customers. Although development teams deliver features more frequently, operations teams struggle to implement them rapidly [51]. After conducting a thorough content analysis, it has been found that DevOps comprises eight key components. DevOps is a development methodology that aims to bridge the gap between Development and Operations teams. The use of DevOps can facilitate communication and collaboration, enable continuous integration and delivery with automated deployment, as well as ensure quality assurance [28].

Leidecker and Bruno [34] stated that *critical success factors* The factors that require proper sustainability, maintenance, or management for a firm to achieve significant success are known as Critical Success Factors. These factors have unique characteristics, conditions, or variables, and they have a positive impact on the firm in a particular industry. A study conducted by Ram et al. [40] suggested that we can name the factors as critical success factors if the factor is addressed in a satisfactory manner that increases the performance of the organization. They also argued that when CSFs are in practice for achieving organizational performance improvements, successful implementation may influence the relationship between CSF and improvements in organizational performance [4–6,8,9,40].

Literature also suggests that team and process efficiency have some impacts on DevOps success [18]. Smite et al. [44] It is suggested that team efficiency suffers due to a reluctance to ask superiors questions and a lack of understanding of the facts. The study suggests that offshore DevOps teams may be hesitant to express criticism in order to seek guidance from their superiors. According to Wiedenmann et al. [50], Cross-functional teams and teams with DevOps skills have a significant impact on organizational success. Tsanos et al. [48] and Kolfschoten [30] claimed that mutuality, trust, commitment, and mutual respect among teams impact the team efficiency for DevOps practices.

5.2   Limitations

In this section, we discuss the threats to the validity of this study in the context of qualitative research [24,31,33]. Transferability. The concept of transferability is essential to determine how applicable our findings are to other settings. To achieve this, we conducted semi-structured interviews with 16 participants from LinkedIn, representing a range of backgrounds. Our research reveals informative and insightful outcomes. However, we must acknowledge that the saturation levels may have differed if the interviews had been conducted in a different sequence.

Credibility. Ensuring the research results were accurate and based on the original data was a priority. To achieve this, we took specific steps to ensure the research was credible. These included reviewing all research steps and discussing the findings several times among the authors to reduce any bias that may have been present in the study or interviews. We also recommend that other researchers validate the themes we have identified in the future, further strengthening the credibility of our findings.

Confirmability refers to the degree to which other researchers can check the findings. We do not have the participants' permission to share the transcripts of the interviews. We identified each success factor and its implications along with professionals' perspectives by quoting participants as far as possible [21].

6   Conclusion

This paper presents a thorough thematic analysis of interviews (N=16) conducted with DevOps professionals to gain valuable insights into the critical factors that impact organizational performance. One of the paper's contributions provides an enhanced definition of DevOps success factor identification for organizational software automation practices. Additionally, the detailed description of DevOps adoption and implementation presented in this paper has shown that fostering a (1) collaborative organizational culture, (2) Integrating DevOps automation, (3) cultivating strong work ethics, (4) addressing challenges related to remote teamwork, and (5) establishing dedicated DevOps security teams are essential factors for better organizational practices. The study provides practical recommendations for organizations to improve their DevOps practices, bridging theory with actionable guidance for practitioners.

References

1. Adolph, S., Hall, W., Kruchten, P.: Using grounded theory to study the experience of software development. Empir. Softw. Eng. **16**, 487–513 (2011)
2. Al-Zahrani, S., Fakieh, B.: How devops practices support digital transformation. Int. J. Adv. Trends Comput. Sci. Eng. **9**(3), 2780–2788 (2020)
3. Almeida, F., Simões, J., Lopes, S.: Exploring the benefits of combining devops and agile. Future Internet **14**(2), 63 (2022)
4. Azad, N.: Understanding devops critical success factors and organizational practices. In: 2022 IEEE/ACM International Workshop on Software-Intensive Business (IWSiB), pp. 83–90. IEEE (2022)
5. Azad, N.: The impact of devops critical success factors and organizational practices (2023)
6. Azad, N., Hyrynsalmi, S.: What are critical success factors of DevOps projects? A systematic literature review. In: Wang, X., Martini, A., Nguyen-Duc, A., Stray, V. (eds.) ICSOB 2021. LNBIP, vol. 434, pp. 221–237. Springer, Cham (2021). https://doi.org/10.1007/978-3-030-91983-2_17
7. Azad, N., Hyrynsalmi, S.: Devops challenges in organizations: through professional lens. In: Carroll, N., Nguyen-Duc, A., Wang, X., Stray, V. (eds.) ICSOB 2022, pp. 260–277. Springer, Cham (2022). https://doi.org/10.1007/978-3-031-20706-8_18
8. Azad, N., Hyrynsalmi, S.: Devops critical success factors-a systematic literature review. Inf. Softw. Technol. 107150 (2023)
9. Azad, N., Hyrynsalmi, S., Mäntymäki, M.: Understanding devops critical success factors: Insights from professionals. In: Janssen, M., et al. (eds.) Conference on e-Business, e-Services and e-Society, pp. 78–90. Springer, Cham (2023). https://doi.org/10.1007/978-3-031-50040-4_7
10. Bamigbala, T.: Data ethics and non-compliance challenges in devops (2023)
11. Bass, L., Weber, I., Zhu, L.: DevOps: A Software Architect's Perspective. Addison-Wesley Professional, Boston (2015)
12. Ben Mesmia, W., Escheikh, M., Barkaoui, K.: Devops workflow verification and duration prediction using non-markovian stochastic petri nets. J. Softw. Evol. Process **33**(3), e2329 (2021)

13. Bezemer, C.P., et al.: How is performance addressed in devops? In: Proceedings of the 2019 ACM/SPEC International Conference on Performance Engineering, pp. 45–50 (2019)
14. Bobrov, E., Bucchiarone, A., Capozucca, A., Guelfi, N., Mazzara, M., Masyagin, S.: Teaching DevOps in academia and industry: reflections and vision. In: Bruel, J.-M., Mazzara, M., Meyer, B. (eds.) DEVOPS 2019. LNCS, vol. 12055, pp. 1–14. Springer, Cham (2020). https://doi.org/10.1007/978-3-030-39306-9_1
15. Bosch, J.: Software product lines: organizational alternatives. In: Proceedings of the 23rd International Conference on Software Engineering, ICSE 2001, pp. 91–100. IEEE (2001)
16. Braun, V., Clarke, V.: Using thematic analysis in psychology. Qual. Res. Psychol. **3**(2), 77–101 (2006)
17. Cruzes, D.S., Dyba, T.: Recommended steps for thematic synthesis in software engineering. In: 2011 International Symposium on Empirical Software Engineering and Measurement, pp. 275–284. IEEE (2011)
18. Díaz, J., Almaraz, R., Pérez, J., Garbajosa, J.: Devops in practice: an exploratory case study. In: Proceedings of the 19th International Conference on Agile Software Development: Companion, pp. 1–3 (2018)
19. Díaz, J., et al.: Harmonizing devops taxonomies-a grounded theory study. J. Syst. Softw. **208**, 111908 (2024)
20. Dikert, K., Paasivaara, M., Lassenius, C.: Challenges and success factors for large-scale agile transformations: a systematic literature review. J. Syst. Softw. **119**, 87–108 (2016)
21. Fernandes, M., Ferino, S., Fernandes, A., Kulesza, U., Aranha, E., Treude, C.: Devops education: an interview study of challenges and recommendations. In: Proceedings of the ACM/IEEE 44th International Conference on Software Engineering: Software Engineering Education and Training, pp. 90–101 (2022)
22. Ford, D., et al.: A tale of two cities: software developers working from home during the covid-19 pandemic. ACM Trans. Softw. Eng. Methodol. (TOSEM) **31**(2), 1–37 (2021)
23. Gall, M., Pigni, F.: Taking devops mainstream: a critical review and conceptual framework. Eur. J. Inf. Syst. **31**(5), 548–567 (2022)
24. Guba, E.G.: Criteria for assessing the trustworthiness of naturalistic inquiries. ECTJ **29**(2), 75–91 (1981)
25. Hamunen, J., et al.: Challenges in adopting a devops approach to software development and operations (2016)
26. Horton, J., Macve, R., Struyven, G.: Qualitative research: experiences in using semi-structured interviews. In: The Real Life Guide to Accounting Research, pp. 339–357. Elsevier (2004)
27. Huttermann, M.: Devops for developers: integrate development and operations. The Agile Way (2012)
28. Jabbari, R., bin Ali, N., Petersen, K., Tanveer, B.: What is devops? A systematic mapping study on definitions and practices. In: Proceedings of the Scientific Workshop Proceedings of XP2016, pp. 1–11 (2016)
29. Kallio, H., Pietilä, A.M., Johnson, M., Kangasniemi, M.: Systematic methodological review: developing a framework for a qualitative semi-structured interview guide. J. Adv. Nurs. **72**(12), 2954–2965 (2016)
30. Kolfschoten, G.L., de Vreede, G.J., Briggs, R.O., Sol, H.G.: Collaboration 'engineerability'. Group Decis. Negot. **19**(3), 301–321 (2010)
31. Korstjens, I., Moser, A.: Series: practical guidance to qualitative research. Part 4: Trustworthiness and publishing. Eur. J. General Pract. **24**(1), 120–124 (2018)

32. Kuusinen, K., Albertsen, S.: Industry-academy collaboration in teaching devops and continuous delivery to software engineering students: towards improved industrial relevance in higher education. In: 2019 IEEE/ACM 41st International Conference on Software Engineering: Software Engineering Education and Training (ICSE-SEET), pp. 23–27. IEEE (2019)

33. Larios Vargas, E., Aniche, M., Treude, C., Bruntink, M., Gousios, G.: Selecting third-party libraries: the practitioners' perspective. In: Proceedings of the 28th ACM Joint Meeting on European Software Engineering Conference and Symposium on the Foundations of Software Engineering, pp. 245–256 (2020)

34. Leidecker, J.K., Bruno, A.V.: Identifying and using critical success factors. Long Range Plan. **17**(1), 23–32 (1984)

35. Leite, L., Pinto, G., Kon, F., Meirelles, P.: The organization of software teams in the quest for continuous delivery: a grounded theory approach. Inf. Softw. Technol. **139**, 106672 (2021)

36. Luz, W.P., Pinto, G., Bonifácio, R.: Building a collaborative culture: a grounded theory of well succeeded devops adoption in practice. In: Proceedings of the 12th ACM/IEEE International Symposium on Empirical Software Engineering and Measurement, pp. 1–10 (2018)

37. Meyer, A.N., Fritz, T., Murphy, G.C., Zimmermann, T.: Software developers' perceptions of productivity. In: Proceedings of the 22nd ACM SIGSOFT International Symposium on Foundations of Software Engineering, pp. 19–29 (2014)

38. Mohan, V., Othmane, L.B.: Secdevops: is it a marketing buzzword?-mapping research on security in devops. In: 2016 11th International Conference on Availability, Reliability and Security (ARES), pp. 542–547. IEEE (2016)

39. Paternoster, N., Giardino, C., Unterkalmsteiner, M., Gorschek, T., Abrahamsson, P.: Software development in startup companies: a systematic mapping study. Inf. Softw. Technol. **56**(10), 1200–1218 (2014)

40. Ram, J., Corkindale, D., Wu, M.L.: Implementation critical success factors (CSFS) for ERP: do they contribute to implementation success and post-implementation performance? Int. J. Prod. Econ. **144**(1), 157–174 (2013)

41. Shahin, M., Babar, M.A., Zahedi, M., Zhu, L.: Beyond continuous delivery: an empirical investigation of continuous deployment challenges. In: 2017 ACM/IEEE International Symposium on Empirical Software Engineering and Measurement (ESEM), pp. 111–120. IEEE (2017)

42. Sjøberg, D.I., Dybå, T., Anda, B.C., Hannay, J.E.: Building theories in software engineering. In: Guide to Advanced Empirical Software Engineering, pp. 312–336 (2008)

43. Skenderi, M., Luma-Osmani, S., Imeri, F.: Ethics in devops, the attitude of programmers towards it. J. Nat. Sci. Math. UT **5**(9–10), 69–85 (2020)

44. Šmite, D., Moe, N.B., Gonzalez-Huerta, J.: Overcoming cultural barriers to being agile in distributed teams. Inf. Softw. Technol. **138**, 106612 (2021)

45. Smith, J.A.: Semi structured interviewing and qualitative analysis (1995)

46. Smolander, K., Rossi, M., Purao, S.: Software architectures: blueprint, literature, language or decision? Eur. J. Inf. Syst. **17**, 575–588 (2008)

47. Strauss, A., Corbin, J.: Basics of Qualitative Research. Sage Publications (1990)

48. Tsanos, C.S., Zografos, K.G., Harrison, A.: Developing a conceptual model for examining the supply chain relationships between behavioural antecedents of collaboration, integration and performance. Int. J. Logist. Manag. (2014)

49. Ur Rahman, A.A., Williams, L.: Security practices in devops. In: Proceedings of the Symposium and Bootcamp on the Science of Security, pp. 109–111 (2016)

50. Wiedemann, A., Wiesche, M., Krcmar, H.: Integrating development and operations in cross-functional teams-toward a devops competency model. In: Proceedings of the 2019 on Computers and People Research Conference, pp. 14–19 (2019)
51. Zarour, M., Alhammad, N., Alenezi, M., Alsarayrah, K.: A research on devops maturity models. Int. J. Recent Technol. Eng **8**(3), 4854–4862 (2019)

Micro-credentials Ecosystem: Dynamic Capabilities Do Matter

Yevgen Bogodistov[1]([✉]) [ID], Petar Despotovic[2] [ID], and Lyubov Stafyeyeva[3] [ID]

[1] Business Administration Online Department, Management Center Innsbruck, Universitätsstraße 15, 6020 Innsbruck, Austria
yevgen.bogodistov@mci.edu
[2] International University Monaco, Le Stella, 14 Rue Hubert Clerissi, 98000 Monaco, Monaco
petar.despotovic@monaco.edu
[3] Learning Solutions Department, Management Center Innsbruck, Universitätsstraße 15, 6020 Innsbruck, Austria
lyubov.stafyeyeva@mci.edu

Abstract. The study explores the perceptions of the micro-credentials software ecosystem (MC-SECO) by higher education institutions (HEIs). Through a discrete choice experiment, we investigate how various dimensions of MC-SECOs influence decision-making processes within HEIs. We aim to understand the factors that facilitate or hinder MC-SECO implementation. Our research highlights the importance of collaboration, risk management, trust, sharing, and transparency in developing a cooperative and efficient ecosystem. Collaboration aiming at enhancing sensing and shaping opportunities and threats, seizing an opportunity, and reconfiguring the resource base (i.e., dynamic capabilities provided by the ecosystem) is crucial for decision-making. In contrast, the willingness to share physical resources is seen as an obstacle in the implementation process. Risk-avoidance strategies dominate HEIs' decision-making. By investigating the preferences and reasons for the resistance of HEIs regarding MC-SECO implementation, this research contributes to the understanding of digital transformation in education, emphasising the need for ecosystems that support dynamic capabilities, openness, and innovation.

Keywords: Micro-Credentials · Ecosystem · Higher Education · Discrete Choice Experiment

1 Introduction

Software ecosystems (SECOs) offer a valuable approach for assembling large-scale software systems through the integration components created by both internal and external stakeholders on a unified software platform [1]. In the educational sector, the ecosystems represent an all-round approach to learning, where innovation in teaching methodologies, technology integration, and partnership models redefine how education is delivered and consumed [2]. For instance, higher education institutions (HEIs) now provide a broader spectrum of formal and informal courses online, which provide unprecedented access to learning opportunities and enable students to participate and earn digital certificates known as "micro-credentials" (MC).

However, MCs are often approached as a tool, needing a connection to the theoretical lens. For instance, MCs are simplified to certification of individuals' precise skill sets or knowledge areas. Yet, MCs are facilitated mainly through digital platforms that bridge educational institutions with external providers [3]. This shift widens the gateway to specialised learning and cultivates a cooperative ecosystem among traditional academic bodies, corporate entities, and standalone educational platforms [4]. Consequently, a more vibrant and interlinked educational framework emerges, positioning micro-credentials as key elements in narrowing the divide between formal education and the rapidly changing job market demands. We, thus, land in the field of dynamic capabilities - a strategic management concept explaining how organisations cope with change [5, 6]. This framework cannot be organised in a siloed way (i.e. at the level of separate universities) and requires interlinkage to other actors, such as students, local authorities, other market players, etc. Hence, to be successful, micro-credentials systems require platforms and the appropriate ecosystem to provide standard interfaces for collaboration, data quality control, sharing of resources, and a certain transparency [7]. Such MC-SECOs leverage dynamic capabilities to foster innovation in educational delivery and credentialing.

In the event of micro-credentials, it is crucial to develop an ecosystem that will be acceptable, efficient, and effective for all involved actors. Given the critical role of the European Union's micro-credentials initiative [8] in promoting inclusion through more adaptable and module-based learning opportunities, understanding the decisive characteristics of an MC-SECO becomes imperative in Europe. Yet, divergence in the interpretation of micro-credentials scope and objectives could lead to conflicts in selecting and applying the appropriate digital solutions. Different aspects of the MC-SECO might be unacceptable for HEIs, who have to implement this system at the end of the day. Our research explores the specifics of the MS-SECO within HEIs. Here, we aim to understand the aspects of the ecosystem that might be perceived as the biggest hurdles in the way to their implementation. We better understand how an MC-SECO can accelerate or decelerate an HEI's dynamic capability. Therefore, we posit the research question:

RQ: "How do different aspects of a micro-credentialing ecosystem influence decision-making processes at HEIs in the context of advancing educational strategies?".

This study contributes to the existing knowledge of software ecosystems by demonstrating how the principles and dynamic capabilities inherent in SECOs can be applied to the development and implementation of micro-credentialing systems.

2 Theoretical Background

2.1 Micro-credential Software Ecosystems

In the age of digital transformation in the higher education sector, SECOs have emerged as complex networks of interdependent entities – universities, students, and industry partners – collaboratively engaging within a shared digital landscape to address both supply and demand challenges [9]. This synergy accelerates innovation and fosters a uniquely collaborative culture, setting the stage for a fluid exchange of knowledge, resources, and opportunities across traditional boundaries that is necessary in a dynamic world, driven by frequency, magnitude, and irregularity of change [10].

Respectively, ecosystems have to remain dynamic to meet the demands of turbulent environments and constantly growing customers' and collaborators' needs and allow for value co-creation [11]. The dynamics of such ecosystems are characterised by their transparency, openness, responsiveness to emerging trends, and the capability to establish trust among all stakeholders [12]. For instance, Alam and colleagues [7] argue that openness builds the basis for creating any software ecosystem while emphasising the strategic importance of leveraging external knowledge and resources across organisational and industry boundaries, promoting the adoption of open innovation models. Additionally, Jansen and colleagues [13] suggest that fostering a sense of community within SECOs for software vendors is critical, ensuring the interconnectedness and mutual dependence of different ecosystem components [14].

These components have to remain open. This openness is a strategy and a fundamental shift in the innovation landscape, transitioning from isolated operations to collaborative, open innovation ecosystems [15]. This approach has reshaped the dynamics of HEIs, encouraging universities, students, and industry partners to engage more deeply in shared, innovative endeavours with a forward-looking perspective on the growth and development of educational technologies and methodologies [16].

In addition, creating an environment of openness in HEIs introduces distinct challenges. The openness paradigm requires a shift in academic culture to one where proprietary knowledge is shared, and collaboration is routine, which may conflict with long-standing institutional practices [17]. For instance, integrating micro-credentials into higher education depends on developing an effective ecosystem that engages various stakeholders and establishes consensus on shared standards and validation processes [8]. Consequently, HEIs must reconsider the established norms and approach the recent technological developments, ensuring they complement and enrich the existing educational models.

2.2 Research Model

Identifying the specific attributes and features of HEIs value in MC-SECOs becomes a critical input for informed decision-making in the HEI sector. Hence, recognising the necessity of a systematic approach to MC-SECO challenges (as perceived by HEIs) becomes essential to ecosystem providers. Be it the EU or a private firm, only knowing what characteristics of the proposed ecosystem HEIs value can they offer a solution that will be accepted, acknowledged, and implemented.

Our research aims to explore the dynamics of collaboration, sharing, risk-taking, trust, and transparency within specific contexts, utilising a discrete choice experiment (DCE). This method allows us to examine the varied perceptions of MC-SECO characteristics and assess the readiness to implement these solutions. As the model for our DCE, we took the open innovation ecosystem model as proposed by Alam and colleagues [7]. This model offers a set of five interrelated dimensions of collaboration, sharing, risk-taking, trust, and transparency. We use these dimensions as attributes, i.e.

independent variable groups, whereby each attribute is approached via a set of variables within the group - the so-called levels.

The integration of these dimensions into our research model directly aligns with the dynamic capability framework [18] and the principles of open innovation ecosystems [7]. Dynamic capabilities, as defined by Teece [18], involve the ability of an organisation to renew and adapt its competencies in response to changing environments. Dynamic capabilities are rooted in three pillars: a capacity to sense and shape opportunities and threats, a capacity to seize an opportunity, and a capacity to reconfigure an organisation's resource base to meet challenges [5].

As Alam et al. (2022) propose that innovation ecosystems facilitate dynamic capabilities through inter-organisational collaboration and innovation, we adopt the model by Teece [5] as one of our attributes in the DCE. In this novel way, we link the dynamic capabilities framework with MC-SECOs in the educational sector.

Additionally, we incorporated two scalable attributes to better understand the importance of each attribute and level. We use "Time for Establishing the Ecosystem" and "Time Saved per Student's Credential" to quantify each participant's preference level. Later, this approach allows us to convert complex relationships into more tangible metrics, e.g. willingness to trade time of establishing the ecosystem to retain a specific aspect. Put differently, we calculate how much educational institutions are willing to invest in fostering specific attributes and levels, similar to the concept of willingness to pay. Our study design is depicted in Fig. 1.

3   Methodology

3.1   Method Selection

Our study utilises a DCE, which combines experimental manipulations (i.e. causality test) with the depth of a questionnaire (i.e. number of items) [19]. This provides us with a robust framework for answering our research question. The DCE is a research method used to indicate an individual's preferences for various features of products or services by letting participants make a simple choice from their varying constellations [20, 21]. It is a specific type of Choice-Based Conjoint analysis that quantitatively assesses how much importance individuals place on different product attributes [22].

This methodological approach draws inspiration from foundational studies on digitalisation [19, 21, 23] and is tailored to investigate how participants prioritise various attributes of the MC-SECO implementation. By examining factors such as trust, collaboration, sharing, risk-taking, and transparency, we can gain insights into the decision-making processes of individuals within the context of HEIs. Each attribute within our study is characterised by multiple levels, providing a detailed understanding of participants' preferences.

3.2   Operationalisation

While developing their model, Alam and colleagues [7] suggest the dimensions and aspects forming these dimensions. Thus, we can use their suggestions for our operationalisation of the model. For instance, the dimension of collaboration is addressed using

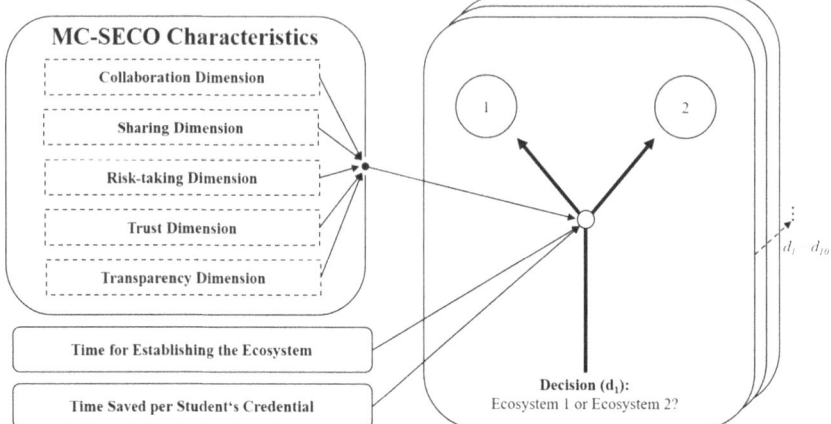

Fig. 1. Study design.

the dynamic capabilities framework. Collaboration among loosely coupled interdependent actors should enhance their ability to respond to environmental change via "unused ideas be available to others" [7]. Following Teece's [5] notion, dynamic capabilities can be disaggregated into capacities to sense and shape opportunities and threats, seize an opportunity, and reconfigure a firm's resource base to implement the selected opportunity. Consequently, we operationalised this dimension using the three sub-dimensions from dynamic capabilities literature, whereby we also added the zero-level value of "No collaboration required".

Interestingly, the dynamic capabilities approach is a perfect fit with the model. Alam and colleagues [7] assume that at the core of the ecosystem lies risk-taking that is correlated with trust, sharing, transparency, and collaboration dimensions. In their groundbreaking paper, Bogodistov and Wohlgemuth [24] introduce dynamic capabilities to risk management. This amalgamation allows us to treat risks holistically, creating the enterprise risk management approach from a siloed approach. In this paper, the scholars provide ways to treat risks common in risk management literature and can be used as levels in our DCE. Namely, there are only four ways to manage risks: avoid them, mitigate them, transfer them (e.g. to an insurer), or accept them [24, 25]. We use the latter option as our zero-level value, as "acceptance" assumes the risks are taken without any additional moves.

We operationalise the trust dimension building on Vergne's [26] classification of types of digital storage within organisations. Here, we extend the framework to the domain of digital platforms for micro-credentials in HEIs. Vergne [26] distinguishes between three types of ecosystem digital platforms: (1) *centralised* systems with a single point of control; (2) *decentralised* systems, which distribute control among multiple entities or locations; (3) *distributed* systems, which spread both control and operational activities across multiple nodes or entities, potentially without a hierarchical structure. Yet, it is not only the degree of centralisation or, put differently, where the control over data happens. Different new technologies, such as blockchain, offer a high level of control and, thus, trust [27–29]. For this reason, we combine the notion of centralisation (centralised vs decentralised vs distributed) with the technology (blockchain-based vs regular data storage on a regular server). This brings us to the six levels for the attribute "trust", whereby the regular data storage with a university's control over data is only used as the zero-level value. Trust approached via control over data quality is also related to risk-taking [e.g. 30] as suggested by the model of Alam and colleagues [7].

The sharing dimension within MC-SECOs is operationalised following the same principle, focusing on the different levels of resource sharing that reflect varying degrees of openness within the ecosystem. We took the classification of resources from Grant and Jordan [31] and introduced levels for sharing physical, intangible, and human resources. "Ecosystem requires no resource sharing" serves as a baseline for our analysis. Resource sharing is also correlated with risk-taking, as it involves opening up resources that institutions might traditionally guard as competitive assets, which aligns with the model by Alam and colleagues [7]. This openness is a double-edged sword, potentially exposing vulnerabilities but also fostering the way for unprecedented collaboration and openness [17].

In our DCE, we approach the essence of transparency through communication concerning different aspects of ecosystem dynamics. In our approach, transparency includes levels of open communication about resource distribution, selection criteria for the credentials, development process, the costs involved, and commercialisation [7]. By fostering open dialogue across these levels, MC-SECOs not only manage inherent risks more effectively but also embrace risk-taking as a strategic opportunity for the growth and efficiency of the SECO [32].

The final list of attributes and levels can be found in Table 1. To simplify the decision-making procedure, we provided participants not with the name of the attribute (e.g. "Risk-taking") but with a statement (e.g. "Risk management strategy is based on..."), whereby levels aim to finalise it (e.g. "Avoiding most risks (e.g. due to alternative solutions)").

In our DCE, a participant ($q = 1, ..., Q$) encounters $j = 2$ alternatives in t decisions. Each participant evaluates his or her expected utility based on the seen alternatives in a tth decision – a combination of different randomly shown levels for each of the attributes. In general form, the utility for the parameters k is described by [21]:

$$U_{jtq} = \sum_{k=1}^{K} \beta_{qk} x_{jtqk} + \varepsilon_{jtq} = \beta_q' X_{jtq} + \varepsilon_{jtq},$$

where X_{jtq} stands for the full vector of observed explanatory variables, including attributes of alternatives and the choice task itself in choice situation t. The components β_q' and ε_{jtq} are not observable and are treated as stochastic influences [33].

3.3 Experimental Procedure

The study utilised the Prolific platform to collect data from English-speaking educational professionals in the European Union, embedding attention checks to ensure data integrity, as recommended by Hauser & Schwarz [34]. The participants were aware of the study's duration and maintained their anonymity by storing their data in a Prolific database, which was inaccessible to our research team. Aware of the potential challenges in collecting data online [35], we implemented multiple attention checks to ensure active engagement from participants, along with demographic questions to verify the sample's alignment with participant reports from Prolific. Participants were briefed about these attention checks, understanding that completion of the study and subsequent compensation depend on passing these checks. Our experiment asked participants to choose between two decision options, as illustrated in Fig. 2. They were required to make ten such choices and pass two attention checks.

3.4 Measures

Our *independent variables* are derived from a comprehensive examination of attributes central to the dynamics of MC-SECOs, as outlined in Table 1. These attributes and the levels within them aim to elucidate the multifaceted nature of MC-SECOs and the impact of each facet on decision-making. Our *dependent variable* is the participant's decision regarding the options provided. This decision reflects the participant's preferences regarding different aspects of MC-SECO. We included in our analysis *control variables* on professional background, gender, age, and familiarity with the concepts of micro-credentials, ecosystems, certification process, risk management, blockchain, and work with students.

3.5 Sample

To test our model, we decided to use Prolific specifically targeting participants from the European Union engaged in the educational sector, either as part of "College University and Adult Education" or within "Another educational industry".

We introduced several attention checks to ensure data integrity [34], subsequently eliminating 39 participants who failed these measures. This resulted in a finalised group of 161 participants, comprising 70 males and 91 females. Within this group, the distribution of roles within their institution was varied: 51 identified as micro-credential consumers, 38 aligned with student affairs and support, 34 were affiliated with academic departments or faculty, 21 worked in administrative and compliance roles, 16 specialised in eLearning and instructional design, 12 were curriculum developers, 11 were involved in marketing, 9 served as IT specialists, 8 identified as external partners, and 4 were legal and compliance officers. Additionally, 21 participants selected "Other" for their role in their institution, not fitting into the predefined categories. The average age of the participants was 33.47 ($SD = 10.20$). The participants stated an average of 8.34 ($SD = 8.21$) years of professional experience. Out of their total professional experience, participants spent an average of 5.48 ($SD = 6.74$) years in the higher education sector. Regarding the highest level of education, 71 participants had a Master's degree, 43 held a Bachelor's degree, 20 had earned a Doctoral degree, 12 were high school graduates, 10 had college education without earning a degree, 3 possessed an associate degree, one possessed less than a high school degree and one obtained a Habilitation/multiple degrees.

Overall, our data sample demonstrates a strong correlation between the personnel structure within the HEI and the various roles associated with the micro-credentialing process.

Table 1. Attributes and levels of the DCE

Question/Attribute	Level 1	Level 2	Level 3	Level 4	Level 5	Level 6
Collaboration via this platform will help…	Sense new opportunities and threats	Seize an appropriate opportunity	Reconfigure your competencies	*Ecosystem assumes no collaboration*		
Trust between parties is established via…	Centralised blockchain-based solution†	Decentralised blockchain-based solution†	Distributed blockchain-based solution†	*Centralised regular database†*	*Decentralised regular database†*	Distributed regular database†
Requires open **communication** about…	Resources distribution (e.g. tools)	Selection criteria (e.g. Public vs. Private Blockchain)	Development process (e.g. conceptualisation)	Direct/indirect costs (e.g. infrastructure)	Commercialisation (e.g. marketing)	*No open communication required*
Ecosystem assumes parties to **share**…	Some physical resources (e.g., equipment)	Some intangible resources (e.g., information)	Some human resources (e.g. skills, know-how)	*Ecosystem requires no resource sharing*		
Risk management strategy is based on…	Avoiding most risks (e.g. due to alternative solutions)	Mitigating/modifying risks (e.g. less risky alternatives)	Transferring/sharing risks (e.g. insurance, hedging)	*Accepting/retaining risks (with all possible losses)*		
Establishing the system takes…	12 months	14 months	16 months	18 months	20 months	…24 months
Time saved for a student's credential	10%	15%	20%	25%	30%	

Note: We use *italics* to indicate the reference value (zero-level), † indicates that the participants also had an example, e.g. for Centralised blockchain-based solution → (information blocks stored on multiple servers, the EU conducts control).

	Ecosystem 1	Ecosystem 2
Time saved for a student's credential is...	20 per cent	20 per cent
Requires open communication about...	Direct/indirect costs (e.g. infrastructure)	No open communication required
Risk management strategy is based on....	Transfering/sharing risks (e.g. insurance, hedging)	Mitigating/modifying risks (e.g. less risky alternatives)
Collaboration via this platform will help ...	Reconfigure your compentences	Ecosystem assumes no collaboration
Ecosystem assumes parties to share...	Ecosystem requires no resource sharing	Some human resources (e.g. skills, know-how)
Trust between parties is established via...	Decentralised blockchain-based solution (information blocks on multiple servers, control is shared among universities)	Centralised regular database (information is stored on the global EU server and controlled by the EU)
Establishing the system would take...	12 months	20 months

○ Ecosystem 1

○ Ecosystem 2

Fig. 2. An example of a DCE decision (Question: Which of the micro-credentialing ecosystems aligns best with your preferences?).

4   Results

4.1   Procedure and Model Goodness

Considering our binary dependent variable (1 indicating a preference concerning the ecosystem and 0 for a lack of it) we applied a logistic regression procedure in IBM® SPSS®. First, we ran Model 1 for the main predictors of preference concerning a MC-SECO. Second, we ran the same model, where we added an interaction of all independent variables with the control variables (Model 2). The R^2 for our model with control variables was .136, whereas the model with main effects showed an R^2 of .084 which is good [19]. The lower levels of R^2 are lower than usually accepted in social sciences as most of the variability happens within the subject, as each participant has to make 10 decisions and the preferences regarding the dependent variable may be relatively stable.

4.2 Interpretation of Results

In logistic regression, we usually use $Exp(B)$ (i.e. odds ratios), indicating the likelihood of preference of the focal level as compared to the reference value. For instance, a value of 1.517 for sensing new opportunities and threats thanks to collaboration indicates that the ecosystem providing this option will be selected 1.5 times more likely as compared to the ecosystem, offering "no collaboration" (reference value). A value close to one indicates a 50:50 chance (i.e. indifference): for instance, sharing human resources (e.g. skills, know-how) shows an $Exp(B) = 1.043$ ($p = .683$) seems to have no impact when selecting an ecosystem as compared to "no resource sharing". An $Exp(B) < 1$, indicates that the option is being avoided. To calculate how much the value is less preferable, one has to divide 1 by the $Exp(B) < 1$. For instance, our participants tended to avoid sharing physical resources (i.e. equipment or financial resources). This level of the attribute "Sharing" would decrease the preference by $1/.791 \approx 1.3$, i.e. it is 1.3 times less likely that the ecosystem offering this option will be preferred over an ecosystem requiring "no resource sharing". The final results can be found in Table 2.

Additionally, we calculated the willingness-to-trade (WtT) coefficients by the formula below, where v indicates the value we want to convert into:

$$WtTv = \frac{logistic\ coefficient\ B\ of\ the\ focal\ level}{logistic\ coefficient\ B\ of\ the\ conversion\ attribute * (-1)} * step\ size$$

This indicator is an analogy of willingness to pay, whereby the payment is made in time, efficiency, or other scalable variable. For instance, the willingness to trade time for a student's credentialing to avoid most risks is -2.6 (WtTTS $= -2.6$). It means that risk avoidance on average is important for our study participants so much that they are willing to give up 2.6% of their time savings for each student to obtain risk avoidance as a characteristic of the ecosystem. Alternatively, they are willing to wait for 4.5 months longer with the ecosystem establishment to avoid most of the risks (WtTTE $= 4.5$). Willingness to Trade is not an additional analysis but just a way to express preferences in an easy-to-understand manner.

4.3 Results

The final results can be observed in Table 2. Due to space limitations and as the control variables did not play a significant role, we decided not to present them as a table. The few significant indicators were the interaction between risk avoidance and familiarity with the certification process ($Exp(B) = 1.337, p = .038$), indicating that certification-familiar participants tended to avoid risks more. They also preferred centralised blockchain-based solutions for certification ($Exp(B) = 1.491, p = .017$). Yet, these solutions were disliked by participants familiar with risk management ($Exp(B) = 0.732, p = .046$). Participants familiar with blockchain preferred decentralised blockchain-based solutions ($Exp(B) = 1.420, p = .038$) who also scored lower regarding risk avoidance ($Exp(B) = 0.749, p = .041$).

Table 2. Impact of different aspects of MC-SECO on the final decision

	B	S.E.	p	Exp(B)	WtTET	WtTTS
Variable: Collaboration (will help…)						
Sense new opportunities and threats	.417	.104	<,001	1.517	3.23	−1.91
Seize an appropriate opportunity	.386	.103	<,001	1.47	2.99	−1.73
Reconfigure your competencies	.262	.104	.011	1.3	2.03	−1.17
Ecosystem assumes no collaboration	-	-	-	-	-	-
Variable: Trust (established via…)						
Centralised blockchain-based solution	.039	.124	.755	1.04	0.30	−0.17
Decentralised blockchain-based solution	.212	.124	.089	1.236	1.64	−0.95
Distributed blockchain-based solution	−.255	.128	.046	0.775	−1.98	1.14
Centralised regular database	.051	.125	.682	1.053	0.39	−0.23
Distributed regular database	−.211	.125	.091	0.81	−1.63	0.95
Decentralised regular database	-	-	-	-	-	-
Variable: Transparency (open **communication** about…)						
Resources distribution	.175	.127	.169	1.191	1.36	−0.78
Selection criteria	.126	.129	.329	1.135	0.98	−0.56
Development process	.05	.128	.694	1.052	0.39	−0.22
Direct/indirect costs	.087	.129	.502	1.091	0.67	−0.39
Commercialisation	.081	.128	.527	1.084	0.63	−0.36
No open communication required	-	-	-	-	-	-
Variable: Sharing (assumes sharing of…)						
Some physical resources (e.g., equipment)	−.235	.102	.022	0.791	−1.82	1.05
Some intangible resources (e.g., information)	.148	.104	.155	1.159	1.15	−0.66
Some human resources (e.g. skills, know-how)	.042	.103	.683	1.043	0.33	−0.19
Ecosystem assumes no resource sharing	-	-	-	-	-	-
Variable: Risk management (is based on…)						
Avoiding most risks	.58	.105	<,001	1.786	4.5	−2.60

(*continued*)

Table 2. (*continued*)

	B	S.E.	p	Exp(B)	WtTET	WtTTS
Mitigating/modifying risks	.539	.105	<,001	1.715	4.18	−2.42
Transferring/sharing risks	.277	.103	.007	1.32	2.15	−1.24
Accepting/retaining risks	-	-	-	-	-	-
Time for establishment	−.129	.018	<,001	0.879	−1	0.58
Time saved for a student's credential	.223	.026	<,001	1.25	1.73	−1
Constant	−.812	.199	<,001	0.444	-	-

Note: WtTTE - Willingness to trade time for establishing the ecosystem, months; WtTTS - willingness to trade time saved per student, per cent; *italics* indicate reference values.

5   Discussion

Our explorative analysis revealed several interesting findings. First, the thought-provoking point was how dynamic capabilities shape the decision-making process. Our participants demonstrated that all dimensions of a dynamic capability (as a result of collaboration within MC-SECO) are crucial, whereby the capacity to sense and shape opportunities and threats appeared to be the most important. Ecosystems at large may be a way to enhance actors' dynamic capabilities to make their organisations swiftly adapt to changing environments to be on the frontline to capture emerging opportunities [7]. This finding also implies that the MC-SECOs users see ecosystems as a source of their flexibility.

At the same time, participants were less willing to share physical resources such as money and equipment with other MC-SECO members. This finding indicates possible collaboration problems. Alam and colleagues [7] assume that the dimensions of the ecosystem model are interrelated, i.e. collaboration might be possible if parties decide to share their resources among other joint activities. Further research should focus on the interaction between dynamic capabilities and the willingness to share physical resources, as dynamic capabilities aim to reconfigure an organisation's resource base [5, 36]. Interestingly, sharing knowledge and information has not been considered a problem. The HEIs may not be ready to give up on the power they feel they are losing because of sharing physical spaces or limited funds, which is their main reason for resisting openness [1].

We were not surprised by our findings concerning risk management: empirical evidence suggests that people are mostly risk-avoidant. This reflects the mainstream risk management tactic in which organisations minimise possible losses and risks [13]. Nevertheless, risk-taking is an opportunity to be explored by MC-SECOs as a competitive tool rather than a threat. A compromise between risk-taking and risk avoidance might be essential for MC-SECO adoption by the HEIs.

We did not find preferences regarding transparency – our participants appeared to be mostly indifferent regarding the information they have to communicate with the collaborators in an MC-SECO. The same applies to trust – we have found only a weak disfavour of distributed systems, be it regular or blockchain-based data storage. Further research, with a focus on different technologies, might be a promising research avenue for researchers of SECOs.

Nevertheless, MC-SECOs are at the forefront of redefining the educational landscape, connecting the principles of open innovation ecosystems with the dynamic world of digital credentialing. Our study significantly advances the theoretical understanding of SECOs, particularly MC-SECOs, by demonstrating how dynamic capabilities drive the decision-making processes. We show what aspects of a MC-SECO user value most, and what aspects would hinder the process of implementation. We show that MC-SECOs are most valued if they enhance the dynamic capabilities of HEIs, especially their sensing capacities. Thereby, we extend the framework proposed by Teece [5] and enrich the open innovation ecosystem concept by highlighting the importance of collaboration, sharing, risk-taking, trust, and transparency in digital credentialing platforms, as proposed by Alam and colleagues [7].

In the context of HEIs, policymakers should prioritise fostering dynamic capabilities using MC-SECOs. Our study provides policymakers with a list of aspects and their value for HEIs. Policymakers, thus, have a list of hurdles and drivers which should allow them to implement policies that will be largely accepted by HEIs. Moreover, they can address the hurdles directly, explain why HEIs need these aspects of an MC-SECO, or frame their policies differently by focusing on drivers and not on hurdles.

6 Limitations and Future Research

Despite valuable insights, our study has several limitations. Firstly, the sample size, consisting of 161 participants from the European Union, may not fully represent the diversity of perspectives globally, limiting the generalizability of the findings to institutions outside the EU. Future research should aim to include a more diverse and larger sample size, encompassing participants from various regions and types of educational institutions globally. This would enhance the generalisability of the findings.

Secondly, the reliance on self-reported data introduces potential biases, as participants might provide socially desirable responses or inaccurately report their experiences. Further research should therefore consider incorporating mixed methods approaches, combining self-reported data with objective measures to mitigate biases.

Thirdly, the study's focus lies on collaboration, sharing, risk management, trust, and transparency within MC-SECOs and may overlooks other influential factors. We encourage researchers to apply our methodology with other SECO-related theoretical frameworks. Expanding the focus to include additional factors such as institutional absorptive capacities, IT capabilities, and financial considerations would provide a more comprehensive understanding of MC-SECO implementation.

Consequently, we encourage researchers to advance our study by introducing new attributes and levels and relating them to the theories we referenced. Dynamic capabilities and the concept of open innovation ecosystems represent promising and critical research areas. Our study merely scratched the surface of these important topics. Further research is urgently needed.

References

1. ul Hassan, U., Curry, E.: Stakeholder analysis of data ecosystems. In: Curry, E., Metzger, A., Zillner, S., Pazzaglia, J.-C., García Robles, A. (eds.) The Elements of Big Data Value, pp. 21–39. Springer, Cham (2021). https://doi.org/10.1007/978-3-030-68176-0_2
2. Bischoff, K., Volkmann, C.K., Audretsch, D.B.: Stakeholder collaboration in entrepreneurship education: an analysis of the entrepreneurial ecosystems of European higher educational institutions. J. Technol. Transf. **43**, 20–46 (2018)
3. Fischer, T., Oppl, S., Stabauer, M.: Micro-credential development: tools, methods and concepts supporting the European approach. In: Wirtschaftsinformatik 2022 Proceedings. aisel.aisnet.org (2022)
4. Resei, C., Friedl, C., Staubitz, T.: Micro-Credentials in EU and Global. https://openhpi-public.s3.openhpicloud.de/pages/research/27kLG703NBaxDgjuaNjOWe/Corship-R1.1c_micro-credentials.pdf. Accessed 11 Dec 2023
5. Teece, D.J.: Explicating dynamic capabilities: the nature and microfoundations of (sustainable) enterprise performance. Strateg. Manage. J. **28**, 1319–1350 (2007)
6. Teece, D.J.: Dynamic capabilities and (digital) platform lifecycles. In: Entrepreneurship, Innovation, and Platforms, pp. 211–225. Emerald Publishing Limited (2017)
7. Alam, M.A., Rooney, D., Taylor, M.: From ego-systems to open innovation ecosystems: a process model of inter-firm openness. J. Prod. Innov. Manage **39**, 177–201 (2022)
8. Council of the European Union: Council Recommendation of 16 June 2022 on a European Approach to Micro-Credentials for Lifelong Learning and Employability. European Commission (2022)
9. Golden, G., Kato, S., Weko, T.: Quality and value of micro-credentials in higher education: preparing for the future. OECD Educ. Policy Perspect. **40**, 34 (2021)
10. Hauschild, S., Knyphausen-Aufsess, Z., Rahmel, M.: Measuring industry dynamics: towards a comprehensive concept. Schmalenbach Bus. Rev. **63**, 416–454 (2011)
11. Jacobides, M.G., Cennamo, C., Gawer, A.: Towards a theory of ecosystems. Strateg. Manage. J. **39**, 2255–2276 (2018)
12. Otto, D., Kerres, M.: Distributed learning ecosystems in education: a guide to the debate. In: Otto, D., Scharnberg, G., Kerres, M., Zawacki-Richter, O. (eds.) Distributed Learning Ecosystems: Concepts, Resources, and Repositories, pp. 13–30. Springer, Fachmedien, Wiesbaden (2023). https://doi.org/10.1007/978-3-658-38703-7_2
13. Jansen, S., Finkelstein, A.: A sense of community: a research agenda for software ecosystems. In: Proceedings International Conference on Software Engineering (2009)
14. Manikas, K., Hansen, K.M.: Reviewing the health of software ecosystems - a conceptual framework proposal, pp. 33–44 (2013)
15. Stummer, C., Kundisch, D., Decker, R.: Platform launch strategies. Bus. Inf. Syst. Eng. **60**, 167–173 (2018)
16. Bejarano, J.B.P., Sossa, J.W.Z., Ocampo-López, C.: Open innovation: a technology transfer alternative from universities. A systematic literature review. J. Open (2023)
17. Li, X., Chen, W., Alrasheedi, M.: Challenges of the collaborative innovation system in public higher education in the era of industry 4.0 using an integrated framework. J. Innov. Knowl. (2023)
18. Teece, D.J., Pisano, G., Shuen, A.: Dynamic capabilities and strategic management. Strateg. Manage. J. **18**, 509–533 (1997)
19. Schwaiger, A., Bogodistov, Y., Beimborn, D.: Seeing the forest for the trees: how abstract thinking fosters digitalization. In: Academy of Management Annual Meeting Proceedings, p. 13333 (2023)

20. Hiligsmann, M., et al.: Patients' preferences for osteoporosis drug treatment: a discrete-choice experiment. Arthritis Res. Ther. **16**, R36 (2014)
21. Bogodistov, Y., Ostern, N.: Digitization at any cost? Willingness to trade efficiency for organizational, human, and relational costs. In: Americas Conference on Information Systems (2019)
22. Hainmueller, J., Hopkins, D.J., Yamamoto, T.: Causal inference in conjoint analysis: understanding multidimensional choices via stated preference experiments. Polit. Anal. **22**, 1–30 (2014)
23. Farrell, W.C., Bogodistov, Y., Mössenlechner, C.: Is academic integrity at risk? Perceived ethics and technology acceptance of ChatGPT. In: AMCIS 2023 Proceedings (2023)
24. Bogodistov, Y., Wohlgemuth, V.: Enterprise risk management: a capability-based perspective. J. Risk Financ. **18**, 234–251 (2017)
25. Purdy, G.: ISO 31000:2009–Setting a new standard for risk management. Risk Anal. **30**, 881–886 (2010)
26. Vergne, J.P.: Decentralized vs. distributed organization: blockchain, machine learning and the future of the digital platform. Organ. Theor. **1**, 2631787720977052 (2020)
27. Holotiuk, F., Pisani, F., Moormann, J.: Radicalness of blockchain: an assessment based on its impact on the payments industry. Technol. Anal. Strateg. Manag. **31**, 915–928 (2019)
28. Schmidt, C.G., Klöckner, M., Wagner, S.M.: Blockchain for supply chain traceability: case examples for luxury goods. In: Voigt, K.-I., Müller, J.M. (eds.) Digital Business Models in Industrial Ecosystems: Lessons Learned from Industry 4.0 Across Europe, pp. 187–197. Springer, Cham, CH (2021). https://doi.org/10.1007/978-3-030-82003-9_12
29. Khacef, K., Benbernou, S., Ouziri, M., Younas, M.: A dynamic sharding model aware security and scalability in blockchain. Inf. Syst. Front. (2023). https://doi.org/10.1007/s10796-023-10380-y
30. Rouhani, S., Deters, R.: Data trust framework using blockchain technology and adaptive transaction validation. IEEE Access. **9**, 90379–90391 (2021)
31. Grant, R.M., Jordan, J.: Foundations of Strategy. Wiley, Chichester, West Sussex (2015)
32. Gatzert, N., Schmit, J.T.: Supporting strategic success through enterprise-wide reputation risk management (2015). https://papers.ssrn.com/abstract=2654295. https://doi.org/10.2139/ssrn.2654295
33. Hensher, D.A.: Identifying the influence of stated choice design dimensionality on willingness to pay for travel time savings. J. Transp. Econ. Policy (JTEP) **38**, 425–446 (2004)
34. Hauser, D.J., Schwarz, N.: Attentive Turkers: MTurk participants perform better on online attention checks than do subject pool participants. Behav. Res. Methods **48**, 400–407 (2016)
35. Lefever, S., Dal, M., Matthíasdóttir, Á.: Online data collection in academic research: advantages and limitations. Br. J. Educ. Technol. **38**, 574–582 (2007)
36. Barreto, I.: Dynamic capabilities: a review of past research and an agenda for the future. J. Manage. **36**, 256–280 (2010)

A Framework for Managing Platforms as Products in IT Organizations

Vitor Serra Mori[1]([✉]) [iD] and Hans-Bernd Kittlaus[2,3] [iD]

[1] FGV EAESP, São Paulo, SP 01313-902, Brazil
vitor.mori@fgv.edu.br
[2] InnoTivum, Rheinbreitbach, Germany
[3] ISPMA e.V, Rheinbreitbach, Germany

Abstract. In this article, we introduce a framework for product planning of software platforms managed as internal products within Corporate Information Technology (IT). This contextualized framework defines inputs, outputs, stakeholders, process interactions, and the teams involved. It was developed based on insights gathered from twelve expert interviews, and an evaluation with professionals and researchers interested in the topic confirmed its increased completeness, usefulness, and intention to use compared to a non-contextualized framework. The framework establishes a shared understanding and facilitates discussions surrounding the management of platforms as internal products in companies whose core business is not directly related to software products. It provides IT organizations with new approaches to technology management that can improve organizational competitiveness.

Keywords: Software Product management · Platforms · Corporate IT · Framework · ISPMA

1 Introduction

Digital transformation drives customer-centricity, prompting Corporate Information Technology (IT) to use thriving technology companies as benchmarks for their ambitions to increase the business impact of technology. Thriving technology companies have a key capability of connecting with customer needs to conceive and manage products [1]. This has gained even more emphasis as current, most successful business models focus on "owning the consumer" [2]. Tech companies that have software products or products with embedded software in their portfolio rely on Product Management to conceive and manage their offerings. Within this field, Software Product Management (SPM) has emerged as a specialized area of research and knowledge.

IT organizations (formerly Corporate IT, or simply IT) operating software to support their businesses have increasingly embraced Product Management to translate business needs into effective technological solutions as a response to their respective competitive situations and manage the applications in their respective portfolios with a longer-term business perspective.

D. Petrik et al. (Eds.): ICDPM 2024, LNBIP 528, pp. 59–74, 2025.
https://doi.org/10.1007/978-3-031-71515-0_5

Product management, typically used for business-related software, can be extended to internal platforms. This shift aligns with the broader transformation goal of enhancing agility and efficiency [3]. By 'platform,' we refer to an innovation platform, defined in [4] as a "technological foundation upon which the owner and other firms develop complementary innovations". In essence, a platform managed as a product treats its users as customers. We'll refer to this approach as a platform-product. Its mission is to create value for both the products' teams and the end users of those products. This approach has the potential to increase speed and reduce the cognitive load on teams [5]. In IT, that typically starts as an internal technological foundation used by a range of internal products. Sometimes that technological foundation is also sold as a product to external customers.

Developing platform products presents an intriguing option as IT strive to become more agile, efficient, and customer-focused. These platforms can streamline development processes, enhance scalability and flexibility, deliver cost savings, and facilitate ecosystem expansion, while also creating opportunities to monetize platform services or features through licensing, subscriptions, or usage-based fees. Additionally, adopting an open-source model for the platform itself can further reduce costs by sharing development efforts with the community and leveraging external contributions.

Using SPM to manage software platforms as products introduces distinct dynamics in IT organizations. Although research in this area is limited, the growing adoption of Product Management practices in IT highlights the need for further investigation. Therefore, it presents a valuable research opportunity to explore how SPM can effectively manage platforms within this context to overcome potential challenges which can impede the IT organization's plans to respond to the organizational demands and maximize its outcomes.

1.1 Aims and Objectives

As IT organizations increase the adoption of product management practices, they often consider using platforms as a strategic option to create value, understanding, discussing, and addressing the specific challenges and needs of managing platforms within SPM is required.

Using a design science approach [6], this research aims to make practical contributions to SPM. It introduces a context-aware framework to understand and facilitate discussions in real-world scenarios of managing platforms as products within IT. Furthermore, the research makes theoretical contributions by identifying context-specific nuances and challenges, thus increasing knowledge of current issues. This understanding can be used to inform practical solutions and drive innovation in SPM. The research is structured around the following research questions: I. When managing software platforms as products within an IT organization, what adjustments should be made to requirements management and release planning in product planning? II. To what extent has the research progressed in creating a context-aware framework after incorporating known adjustments into its design?

2 Theory on SPM and Platform Products

2.1 Software Product Management (SPM)

Product management gained a particular line of study for applying it to software products in the early 2000s [1, 17–20]. Its early definition was "a well-organized process of processing issues related to requirements, products, and releases" [20]. Its origins have been attributed to organizations such as Microsoft, which invested in this capability in the 90s and has contributed to this development as part of its success [21]. Thus, Microsoft became a reference for the potential results of these practices, among many other organizations that stand out with successful products in the tech universe. The economic success of a product is the goal of product management [19].

Existing research on the subject includes frameworks [19, 20], differences with other practices such as project management [22], bibliographical research [18], the role of the software product manager [23], and adoption processes, impacts, and benefits [1, 17]. One preeminent resource for SPM nowadays is the International Software Product Management Association (ISPMA®), an open, non-profit association of experts, researchers, and industrial professionals fostering SPM excellence across industries. They maintain the SPM body of knowledge as an evolving collection of information and best practices to support product managers and their organizations in addressing their needs to manage software and software-intensive products. One of the most important artifacts they maintain is the ISPMA SPM framework (See appendix B), which shows the full spectrum of SPM tasks in a structured way.

SPM is an area requiring more research coverage, especially when compared to the abundance of knowledge for software development or related practices such as project management. One conclusion raised by the most recent SPM bibliographic research is that the "SPM field is not sharing a coherent set of intellectual background, nor it is too heavily connected to general product management or new product development literature" [18]. The study points to a limitation in that different terminology should be verified, which introduces challenges in estimating the total universe of research around SPM.

What are the advantages of institutionalizing SPM? One study concluded that it's consistent practice supported by training increases the success rate of initiatives in terms of schedule predictability, quality, and duration of projects (time to market) [17]. A subsequent complementary study highlighted the impacts of efficiency gains and execution costs, which are around 20% per year [22]. Despite its limited research on the advantage, it has been recognized as a game changer for technology companies like Amazon AWS [4] and Microsoft [21].

2.2 SPM and Platform Products

Are there specific needs for managing software platforms as products? [19] states that product management applies wholly to a platform product. There are limited studies on the subject, according to the most recent bibliographic research on SPM [18], and those that exist reinforce that systematic management of the process is necessary to capture the benefits, coordinating the needs of different stakeholders.

This suggests that while nuanced approaches are crucial for platform product management, existing frameworks do not explicitly outline these nuances. Instead, they emerge in the practical application of these frameworks. For instance, when analyzing customers, platform product managers must consider not only their client products' teams as "customers," but also the end-users of those products and their specific contexts. This observation directly supports the study hypothesis, which proposes the development of a contextualized framework to elucidate these nuances.

2.3 SPM in Corporate IT

In an analysis of case studies on digitalization [24], the authors argue that organizations aiming to thrive in the digital age must leverage digital technologies, rethink their business models, and transform. This requires reevaluating business processes, organizational structures, and most importantly, IT management. By doing so, organizations can better align with evolving customer needs and business models.

Digital transformation has spurred increased IT investments and utilization, as it shapes consumer expectations regarding perceived value and access to technologies previously limited to large corporations [25]. Managing structural change and organizational barriers is key to maximizing the value derived from transformation [25].

Generating greater business value requires a deeper understanding of its drivers. Product management is one practice that aids in identifying customer problems, addressing them from a business perspective, and driving value creation [19]. IT organizations have recognized product management as a pathway for continuous evolution, with projections estimating 70% adoption by 2024 [26]. Notably, ISPMA's SPM Foundation syllabus (v1.3) includes an addendum addressing SPM in Corporate IT, offering additional perspectives on its application.

2.4 Reference Framework Selection and Research Focus

We have selected the Utrecht Framework [20] (see Appendix A) as a reference framework, acknowledging its limitation to product planning compared to the full spectrum of SPM tasks [19]. However, by using this first published SPM framework, we create an opportunity for contributors to play a vital role in shaping the framework's development, encouraging their input, and fostering a more detailed and collaborative outcome than if it were initially more fully elaborated.

Due to research constraints, the study focused on two specific areas of interest within the framework: requirements management and release management. These areas emerged as the most relevant for the study context through discussions with SPM researchers. Additionally, the challenges IT organizations often face in balancing stakeholder needs and prioritization further support the focus on these two areas.

For clarity and conciseness, we will refer to the Utrecht Framework simply as the 'reference framework' for the remainder of this discussion, while the framework being developed in this study is called "contextualized framework".

2.5 Research Approach

As a general research goal of advancing theory while providing practical contributions, design-science paradigm had a perfect match as it aims increase knowledge and understanding of a problem domain and produce solutions [7]. This paradigm is widely used and accepted in IT research. Design Science Research (DSR) offers a method for researching to create artifacts [6] and it was selected for its focus on addressing specific business problems [7] and creating "useful things" [8], aligned with the research goals. The artifact in this study is a framework.

Following a Design Science Research Methodology (DSRM) for Information Systems Research [9], the research was divided into two phases: a qualitative phase to create an improved framework, followed by a quantitative phase to evaluate the improved framework (see Fig. 1). The specific research steps for each phase will be described next.

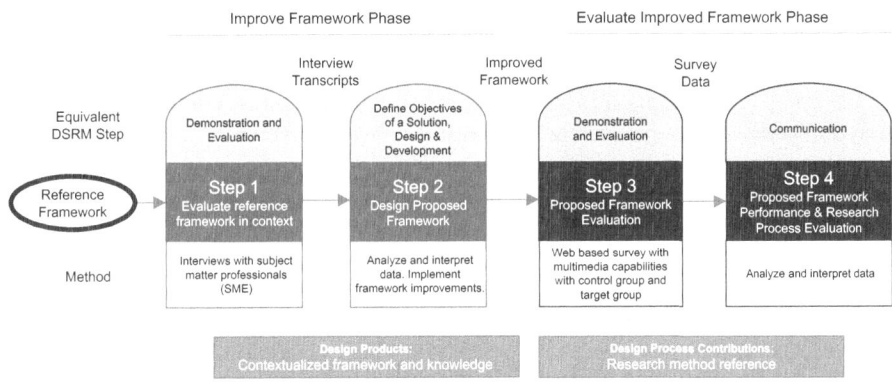

Fig. 1. Research design described in phases and steps for each phase adapted from the DSRM Process Model with a Design & Development Centered Initiated entry point [9]

Evaluate Reference Framework in Context: Produce Knowledge Base

To develop an improved framework, it's essential to first establish a knowledge base on the specific areas needing enhancement. Citing expert opinions through interviews is a well-established research method, particularly valuable in the conceptual stage of artifact evaluation [10]. Interviews serve as a primary data collection tool, enabling researchers to gather rich, qualitative insights from experts regarding their practices, beliefs, experiences, and opinions [11].

Semi-structured interviews were conducted with corporate IT professionals with experience managing software platforms (subject matter experts, or SMEs). The goal was to evaluate a reference framework (ex-ante) and specifically to 1) Assess its completeness, 2/ Determine its helpfulness in real-world settings for representing their professional activities managing platforms and 3/ Gather suggestions for improvements and future work.

Framework Improvement: Design a Contextualized Framework Proposal Using the Produced Knowledge Base

Qualitative data analysis of the interviews followed six steps [12]: 1) organize and prepare data for analysis, 2) get a general sense and engage in reflection by reading all data, 3) conduct a detailed analysis in a coded way, meaning that the data becomes systematically organized and categorized using a coding scheme. 4) build initial description from the coded material, 5) describe and present themes in the qualitative narrative, and 6) interpret data. This interpretation, combined with a literature review, the authors' thematic expertise, and experience with IT artifacts, led to a proposed action plan for improvements and the design of a new framework.

Improved Framework Evaluation: How the Proposed Framework Performs in Comparison to the Reference Framework

The proposed framework was evaluated using a web-based online survey, a method suitable for evaluation studies [13]. This approach offers access to unique populations in a time-efficient and cost-effective way [14]. The target audience included the same SMEs who participated in the earlier interviews as the control group and professionals and researchers interested in the research topic.

One challenge of evaluating a framework through an online survey is ensuring that respondents fully understand the framework before answering. A previous research project examined a multimedia web-based evaluation of an artifact similar to a framework in comparable settings [15], including a naturalistic, ex-post evaluation. This prior study informed the design of both the current survey and the custom survey tool. The design process incorporated crucial lessons and recommendations from the previous study, which were carefully followed in the development of the present study's survey tool.

Proposed Framework Performance: How Much Progress Was Made

To track the research progress, a quantitative analysis was undertaken, with the following hypothesis serving as a guiding metric for measuring progress:

H1: If completeness and usefulness are positively correlated, then intention to use will increase.

The following steps were taken: 1/ Perform a statistical review of the data, including an assessment of reliability and validity, 2/ Analyze the results, focusing on understanding the perception results for each evaluated framework, 3/ Compare the results to a control group.

Final Research Approach Considerations

The research used a mixed methods design with a qualitative phase followed by a quantitative phase. A seven-step process [16] guided the sampling, ensuring adequate sample sizes for each phase. Prospective participants reviewed and electronically signed informed consent forms, which detailed privacy and confidentiality terms, before being allowed to participate. Ethical guidelines from the researcher's institution and relevant literature were followed, with approval from FGV university's Ethical Committee. Additional research design and DSR aligned results reporting can be found in https://aws3.link/HNJJNW.

3   Results

This section briefly describes the process that led to the creation of the SPM Framework for managing platforms as products in IT Organizations, following the research methodology described previously.

Evaluate the Reference SPM Framework in the Context of an IT Organization

Twelve Platform Product Managers or equivalent participated in one-hour interviews. The interviews covered introduction, context awareness, and evaluation of the reference framework. Participants were shown a demonstration of the framework before evaluation. The interview script was refined through dry runs. Participants were recruited through direct contact on LinkedIn. A descriptive summary of the interviews is presented in Table 1.

Table 1. Descriptive Summary of Interview Participants

Characteristic	Description
Organization level	1x Senior Director, 5x Directors, 3x Senior Managers and 3x Managers
Industries Represented	Real State, Retail, Healthcare, Media, Financial services, Insurance and Telecom
Years of experience	All of them with more than one year of experience, average 2.5 years managing of platform as products inside IT Organization
Subject expertise confirmation	All participants provided meaningful details to classify software they managed as a platform-product
Previous Knowledge on SPM Frameworks	Nine respondents stated they were not aware of any specific SPM frameworks. Two mentioned using the Scaled Agile Framework (SAFe) for managing software products, and one indicated their organization had developed its own proprietary SPM framework, which was not shared with the researcher

Participants were managing a diverse range of platforms as products. These included four data platforms, three integration platforms (for e-commerce ecosystem enablement, API management, and low-code integration), and one sales platform offering full business autonomy for product and service configuration, such as pricing, terms, and recurrency. Additionally, they managed a platform general purpose "admin" module to expedite application development, an observability platform, a developer experience platform, and a multi-business sales campaign platform.

Following the interview script, the researcher, as interviewer ensured all questions were covered while allowing for richer discussions that unveiled new perspectives.

Development of a Contextualized SPM Framework – Platforms and IT Organizations

All interview transcripts were loaded into a qualitative data analysis tool [27] to better analyze the data. To identify recurring themes within the transcripts, we conducted a thematic analysis [28] for doing the deductive reasoning. The elaborated themes where formulated based on existing research and are presented in Table 2.

Table 2. Deductive Coding Structure

Group	Codes
Framework Section	Framework-Wide, Requirements Management, Release Planning
Perspective	Stakeholders, Outputs, Inner Flow, Inputs
Evaluation Dimension	Intention to Use, Usefulness, Completeness
Evaluation Direction	☑ Support, ☒ Oppose

During the thematic analysis, inductive reasoning revealed five additional relevant themes within the data: IT context, delivery methodology, terminology, product vs platform boundaries, and intersection with other processes. The coding of items was largely objective, except for evaluation direction, which demanded researcher interpretation. Summarized results are presented in Table 3.

Table 3. Summary of interviews for reference framework evaluation, per characteristic, with sample prominent comments, following DSR evaluation reporting structure [29] from 12 participants

Perceived Completeness	☑ 9	☒ 72
"All entries are relevant... but depending on scope, may not be necessary"		".. just gathering inputs for the product is not enough … it is required some sort of research process, deeper understanding of the customer needs, to include discovery and validation activities, like focus groups, …."
Perceived Usefulness	☑ 7	☒ 5
"How much to fund, I spend a lot of time pitching , what we are asking for the future…. Politics and dynamics… significant part is for maintaining the product"		".. more fluid process less rigid..."
Intention to Use	☑ 30	☒ 28
"If I had more product management knowledge, like this SPM framework, I would have made fewer mistakes and achieving more success"		"… makes sense from a conceptual point of view, but that's not how the world works. For example, we have a very mature release planning framework, much more complex and impactful that the one we are discussing."

Analysis of interview data led to the formulation of solutions that were used to design an improved framework. These solutions were directly linked to specific comments to ensure complete coverage, resulting in the improvement plan.

A proposed contextualized SPM framework was developed through a rigorous analysis of the data. Leveraging prior framework design experience and Microsoft PowerPoint templates, the researcher conducted multiple reviews of transcripts and coded data to ensure the framework's comprehensiveness. Feedback from two other SMEs was incorporated into the final version (Fig. 2). A guided version with detailed process inputs and outputs is provided in https://aws3.link/SQkiMy.

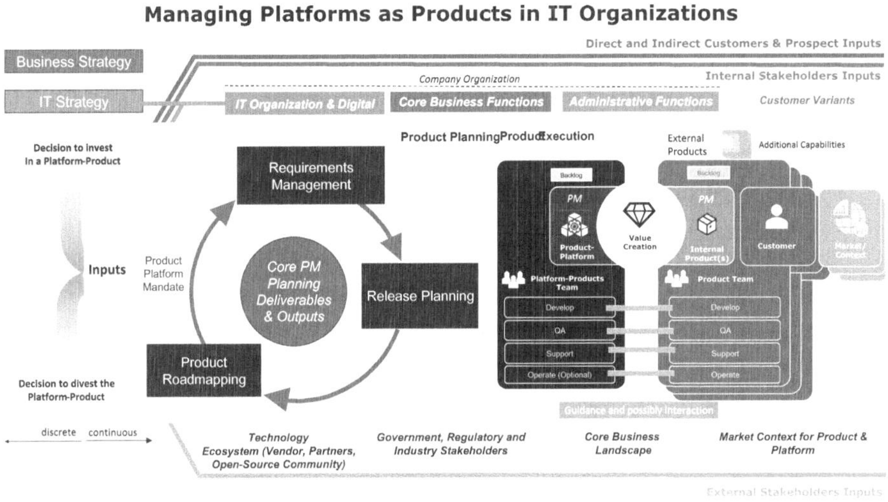

Fig. 2. Contextualized SPM Framework

The contextualized framework entails a product management representation that prioritizes adaptability, value creation, and seamless integration across all stakeholders. This evolved approach reimagines portfolio management by implementing a "Mandate" concept: a holistic blueprint for each platform-product that outlines purpose, funding, and success metrics.

Requirements management transforms into a catalyst for value creation, forging connections between customer needs, potential solutions, and their impact on the business. Prioritization becomes multi-dimensional, balancing value with resource constraints. Release management extends beyond delivery, ensuring adoption and ongoing usage through capabilities like dependency mapping.

The framework itself becomes fluid and continuous, with activities occurring concurrently and iteratively. Stakeholders are viewed contextually, their roles evolving based on organization specifics. A clear distinction is drawn between the platform-product team and the IT organization. Customers are seen as part of a "chain," each with unique needs. The platform-product is differentiated from the client products it serves, recognizing their distinct requirements. Operational needs are woven into the framework, connecting the platform-product with its dependents.

This new framework transcends traditional models, embracing change as a constant. It champions continuous value delivery, collaborative decision-making, and the flexibility to adapt to the ever-shifting demands of the software landscape.

Contextualized SPM Framework–Evaluation and Performance

A web-based survey was used to collect participant evaluations of both the reference framework and the proposed contextualized framework. Evaluations were completed sequentially within the same session.

The survey tool, including instructional videos and allowing user interaction with the frameworks (see https://aws3.link/HNJJNW), was administered from May 23 to June 9, 2023. Thirty participants from five countries completed the survey. Recruitment via LinkedIn resulted in a 2.8% conversion rate. Participants were divided into two groups: those who contributed to the proposed framework, and those who did not. Valid responses met predetermined criteria. Statistical analysis revealed positive impacts, and scale reliability was confirmed. Content validity was ensured.

Contextualized SPM Framework – Performance

The contextualized outperformed the reference in terms of perceived completeness, usefulness, and user intention. User perception and engagement improved, with more users finding the framework complete and useful. Intention to use the framework also increased slightly, with a majority of respondents expressing strong intent. (see Fig. 3).

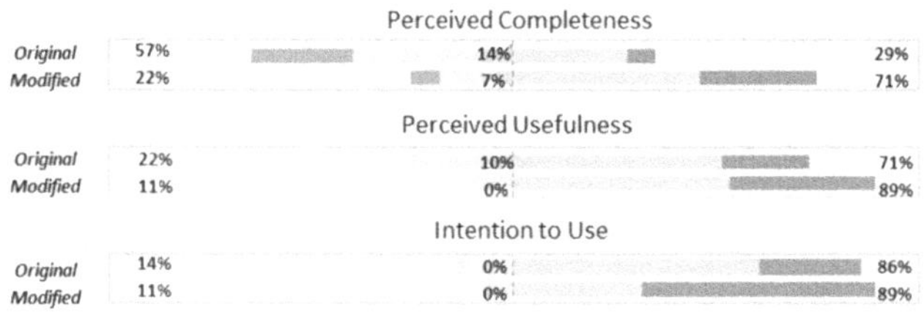

Fig. 3. Survey evaluation - Likert response distributions by each evaluated framework

Cohort analysis revealed that both groups experienced increased intention to use (see Fig. 4). Overall, the contextualized framework better satisfies users' needs, leading to higher satisfaction and increased likelihood of adoption.

Fig. 4. Cohort Evaluation, average score increment

Linear regression analysis was used to predict the intention to use for the two frameworks. Results showed the contextualized framework was 34.7% more accurate than the reference framework, emphasizing the importance of completeness and usefulness in predicting intention to use. This serves as evidence of progress, though further investigation is need. (see Fig. 5).

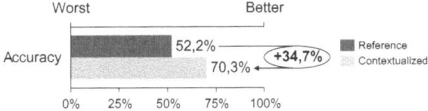

Fig. 5. Framework Improvement Progress

4   Discussion

This study examined prescriptive knowledge within the field of SPM. Practitioners insights were gathered and analyzed, yielding three key areas of discussion. First, we compare our findings with the reference framework to understand how organizations currently implement SPM in practice, particularly within the specific context of our study. Second, we contrast the contextualized framework (developed from the gathered insights) with widely accepted best practices in SPM. Finally, we present additional noteworthy findings from the study.

4.1   Reference Framework Comparison

Completeness Dimension

The interviews focused on the importance of understanding and representing diverse customer needs, both internally and externally. Funding discussions emphasized the need for alignment with objectives and tracking financial performance. Creating a "Platform Product Mandate" serves as a baseline for evaluation. Effective client success management, prioritization, and frequent customer interaction are crucial. Involving customers in discovery and co-creation sessions adds value. Collaboration within IT, considering distribution methods, and life cycle decisions are vital for platform evolution and deployment.

Usefulness Dimension

The framework should be improved to be more useful and align with modern practices. It should be modular and agile, using incremental roadmaps and flexible release strategies. It should also have clear, context-specific terms for stakeholders.

Intention to use Dimension

The intention to use dimension focuses on core product management activities and emphasizes proactive decision-making and stakeholder engagement to ensure product releases deliver value and usage. It encourages using roadmapping to showcase value through impact metrics and linking product management to business outcomes. Additionally, it recommends engaging with business areas through activities like quarterly reviews to highlight the platform's impact and identify opportunities.

4.2   Relationship Between ISPMA's and Contextualized SPM Framework

Within the five areas of ISPMA's product planning, the contextualized framework covers three: roadmapping, release planning, and product requirements engineering. While customer insight isn't explicitly represented, the data gathered and described as "customer inputs" in the contextualized framework aligns with ISPMA's definitions. Notably,

IT organizations typically lack internal customer insight capabilities. Its absence in the contextualized framework raises questions about ownership: Who will be responsible, and how can this competence be developed? On the platform side, product managers heavily rely on collaboration, and it's generally beneficial to have products managed by SPM before platform development begins.

The second area not explicitly defined is Product Life Cycle Management (PLCM). The contextualized framework integrates PLCM with the overall IT strategy, which historically aligns with business strategy and focuses on IT delivery supporting business goals. Investment decisions (start, continue, stop) are often broader enterprise choices and thus "embedded." This highlights the crucial, but potentially insufficient, connection between platform strategy and business strategy, especially regarding short-term financial responses to economic pressures. ISPMA outlines six PLCM phases, but our analysis suggests narrower phases for internal platforms: business case study and formulation, followed by conception, creation, and then a combined market introduction and growth phase (focused on internal software products using the platform). This is followed by maturity, decline, and potential withdrawal (which could occur before decline as a platform migration strategy).

4.3 Others

The research primarily focused on Product Planning in SPM, but also revealed key findings in other areas. In Strategic Management, it was found that market analysis is rarely conducted in IT organizations except for sourcing decisions, and the type of analysis needed for platforms might not be the organization's focus. Product analysis for platforms requires a unique perspective due to their long-term impact on business performance, and IT organizations are not used to evaluating performance linked to specific products.

In Product Strategy, while positioning, product definition, delivery model, service strategy, ecosystem management, and financial management are covered in the contextualized framework, pricing is mainly relevant for externally sold platforms, which were rare in the research sample. Internal pricing was more of a funding scheme than market driven. IT departments struggle with managing costs at the product level, and commercializing platforms externally is rare and requires dedicated sales and marketing roles. The "make or buy" decision depends on software engineering capabilities. Acquiring a platform limits influence on its roadmap but still offers value generation through SPM. Outsourcing the entire platform creation process wasn't a path chosen by any of the interviewed SMEs.

Legal & Intellectual Property Rights (IPR) management is crucial for externally sold platforms. Performance management focuses on linking platform performance to business performance, with metrics prioritizing efficiency over revenue. Investment decisions differ when the product isn't a direct revenue source, posing a risk for platform continuity. Risk management should be developed as a specific capability.

5   Conclusion and Future Work

Contributions for Research and Practice

This study developed a contextualized framework for SPM to provide clarity and guidance specifically tailored for IT organizations managing software platforms as products. The practical value of the framework has been demonstrated by the expressed interest of professionals working within this context in utilizing it over non-contextualized alternative, as well as through observed increases in measures of completeness and usefulness compared to the same non-contextualized alternative. However, limitations exist, including the framework's prescriptive nature, which may not apply to all situations due to its context-dependence; its effectiveness and validity, which have not been tested; and the small sample size and geographic concentration of participants, which limit the reliability and generalizability of the findings. Additionally, the research does not cover all aspects of product planning. Note that while design research informing this study should include design theory contributions, those related to this study will be published separately.

Future Work

In the context of applying SPM to IT, several avenues for future work can enhance this project. First, extend the research by evaluating the contextualized framework along two key dimensions: efficacy, assessing the extent to which the framework achieves its intended outcomes, and validity, ensuring that the framework functions correctly. An action-research approach would be well-suited for this evaluation, allowing for iterative refinement and validation. Second, investigate areas where IT organizations may not fully utilize SPM. This paper highlights specific areas, such as customer insight, where SPM could be better leveraged. Research could help identify and address these gaps, accelerating the adoption of SPM best practices. Third, conduct a more comprehensive study within the IT context. Explore topics such as operating models, roles and responsibilities, methods for estimating platform potential, specific platform types (e.g., data platforms), and how SPM can be adapted based on company size. Additionally, examine the differences between platforms built from scratch versus those extended from existing projects. Finally, enhance executive decision-making for software platform investments with research that helps assess potential return on investment (ROI), considering both financial implications and risks. This can accelerate and substantially improve the quality of decision-making in this crucial area.

Acknowledgments. To everyone who participated in the research, with their contributions, especially the twelve professionals interviewed in the qualitative stage.

Appendix A – Utrecht SPM Framework

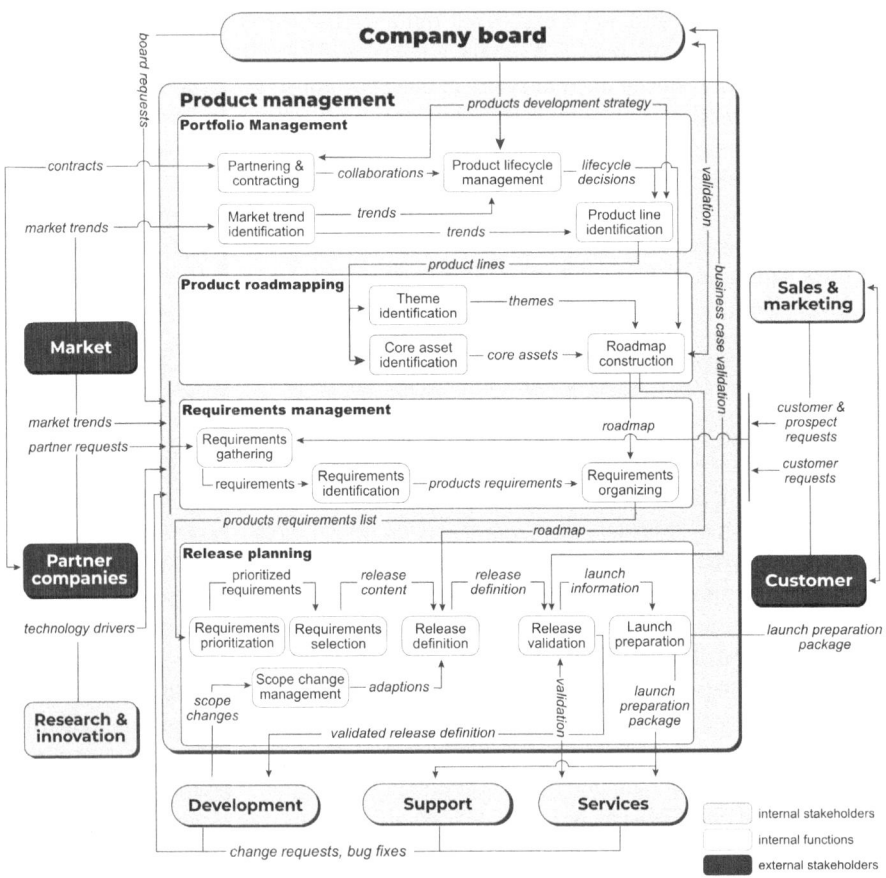

* Note – "The image above is a vector reproduction of the original image published in [20], which was of inadequate quality for use in this research.

Appendix B – ISPMA SPM Framework (V.2.0, 2021)

Strategic Management	Product Strategy	Product Planning	Development	Marketing	Sales and Fulfillment	Delivery Services and Support
Corporate Strategy	Positioning and Product Definition	Customer Insight	Product Architecture Management	Marketing Planning	Sales Planning	Service Planning and Preparation
Portfolio Management	Delivery Model and Service Strategy	Product Life Cycle Management	Development Environment Management	Value Communication	Customer Relationship Management	Service Execution
Innovation Management	Ecosystem Management	Roadmapping	Development Execution	Product Launches	Operational Sales	Technical Support
Resource Management	Sourcing	Release Planning	User Experience Design	Opportunity Management	Operational Fulfillment	Operations
Compliance Management	Pricing	Product Requirements Eng	Detailed Requirements Engineering	Channel Preparation		
Market Analysis	Financial Management		Quality Management	Operational Marketing		
Product Analysis	Legal and IPR Management					
	Performance and Risk Management					ISPMA
Participation	Core		Orchestration			

Activity under SPM responsibility   Activity under other function's responsibility   ISPMA reference architecture v.2

References

1. Ebert, C., Brinkkemper, S.: Software product management – an industry evaluation. J. Syst. Softw. **95**, 10–18 (2014). https://doi.org/10.1016/j.jss.2013.12.042
2. Montgomerie, J., Roscoe, S.: Owning the consumer-getting to the core of the Apple business model. Account. Forum **37** (2013). https://doi.org/10.1016/j.accfor.2013.06.003
3. Harland, P.E., Uddin, Z., Laudien, S.: Product platforms as a lever of competitive advantage on a company-wide level: a resource management perspective. RMS **14**, 137–158 (2020). https://doi.org/10.1007/s11846-018-0289-9
4. Cusumano, M.A.: The cloud as an innovation platform for software development. Commun. ACM **62**(10), 20–22 (2019). https://doi.org/10.1145/3357222
5. Skelton, M., Pais, M.: Team topologies: organizing business and technology teams for fast flow. It Revolution (2019)
6. Dresch, A., Lacerda, D.P., Antunes, J.A.V.: Design science research. In: Design Science Research, pp. 67–102. Springer, Cham (2015). https://doi.org/10.1007/978-3-319-07374-3_4
7. Hevner, M., Park, R.: Design science in information systems research. MIS Q. **28**, 75 (2004). https://doi.org/10.2307/25148625
8. Wieringa, R.: Design science as nested problem solving. In: Proceedings of the 4th International Conference on Design Science Research in Information Systems and Technology - DESRIST 2009, p. 1. ACM Press, New York, USA (2009)
9. Peffers, K., Tuunanen, T., Rothenberger, M.A., Chatterjee, S.: A design science research methodology for information systems research. J. Manag. Inf. Syst. **24**, 45–77 (2007). https://doi.org/10.2753/MIS0742-1222240302
10. Wieringa, R.J.: Design Science Methodology: For Information Systems and Software Engineering. Springer, New York (2014). https://doi.org/10.1007/978-3-662-43839-8
11. Harrell, M.C., Bradley, M.A.: Data collection methods. In: Semi-Structured Interviews and Focus Groups (2009)
12. Creswell, J.W., Cresswell, D.: Research Design: Qualitative, Quantitative, and Mixed Methods Approaches (2018)

13. Siva, M., Nayak, D.P., Narayan, K.A.: Strengths and weaknesses of online surveys. IOSR J. Hum. Soc. Sci. (IOSR-JHSS) **24**, 31–38 (2019)
14. Wright, K.B.: Researching internet-based populations: advantages and disadvantages of online survey research, online questionnaire authoring software packages, and web survey services. J. Comput.-Mediated Commun. **10**(3) (2005). https://doi.org/10.1111/j.1083-6101. 2005.tb00259.x
15. Brandtner, P., Helfert, M.: Multi-media and web-based evaluation of design artifacts-syntactic, semantic, and pragmatic quality of process models. Syst. Signs Actions Int. J. Inf. Technol. Action Commun. Workpractices **11**, 54–78 (2018)
16. Onwuegbuzie, A.J., Collins, K.M.T.: A typology of mixed methods sampling designs in social science research. Qual. Rep. **12**, 281–316 (2007)
17. Ebert, C.: The impacts of software product management. J. Syst. Softw. **80**, 850–861 (2007). https://doi.org/10.1016/j.jss.2006.09.017
18. Hyrynsalmi, S., Suominen, A., Seppanen, M.: A bibliographical study of software product management research. In: 2021 IEEE International Conference on Engineering, Technology, and Innovation, ICE/ITMC 2021 - Proceedings. Institute of Electrical and Electronics Engineers Inc. (2021)
19. Kittlaus, H.-B.: Software Product Management –The ISPMA-Compliant Study Guide and Handbook, 2nd edn. Springer, Heidelberg (2022). https://doi.org/10.1007/978-3-662-65116-2
20. van de Weerd, I., Brinkkemper, S., Nieuwenhuis, R., et al.: Towards a reference framework for software product management. In: 14th IEEE International Requirements Engineering Conference (RE 2006), pp. 319–322. IEEE (2006)
21. Cusumano, M.A., Selby, R.W.: Microsoft Secrets: How the World's Most Powerful Software Company Creates Technology, Shapes Markets, and Manages People. Simon and Schuster (1998)
22. Ebert, C.: Software product management. IEEE Softw. **31**(3), 21–24 (2014). https://doi.org/ 10.1109/MS.2014.72
23. Maglyas, A., Nikula, U., Smolander, K.: What are the roles of software product managers? An empirical investigation. J. Syst. Softw. **86**, 3071–3090 (2013). https://doi.org/10.1016/j. jss.2013.07.045
24. Urbach, N., Röglinger, M.: Introduction to Digitalization Cases: How Organizations Rethink Their Business for the Digital Age, pp. 1–12 (2019)
25. Vial, G.: Understanding digital transformation: a review and a research agenda. J. Strateg. Inf. Syst. **28**, 118–144 (2019). https://doi.org/10.1016/j.jsis.2019.01.003
26. Gartner: Building Product Management Teams in IT and Beyond, Part 1: Structure, Leadership and Roles (2022). https://www.gartner.com/document/3987433. Accessed 29 June 2022
27. Delve: Qualitative Data Analysis Software (SaaS Version) [Computer soft-ware]. https://del vetool.com/
28. Braun, V., Clarke, V.: What can "thematic analysis" offer health and wellbeing researchers? Int. J. Qual. Stud. Health Well-Being **9**(1) (2014). https://doi.org/10.3402/qhw.v9.26152
29. Shrestha, A., Cater-Steel, A., Toleman, M.: How to communicate evaluation work in design science research? An exemplar case study. In: Proceedings of the 25th Australasian Conference on Information Systems, ACIS (2014)

A Conceptual Analysis of Emerging 6G Ecosystem

Nan Yang$^{(\boxtimes)}$ (ID), Sami Hyrynsalmi (ID), and Dominik Siemon (ID)

LUT University, Mukkulankatu 19, 15210 Lahti, Finland
{nan.yang,sami.hyrynsalmi,dominik.siemon}@lut.fi

Abstract. Research on the sixth-generation wireless communication technology (6G) ecosystem has attracted significant attention and captured widespread interest in the past 5 years since 2018. The concept of 6G ecosystem and its related concepts become widely used but have encountered the challenge of ambiguity and misuse due to a lack of rigorous conceptual analysis. To bridge this gap, this paper proposes a novel conceptual analysis framework to explore the components, related concepts, sub-concepts, antecedents, and consequences of 6G ecosystem through a systematic and comprehensive literature review. Our findings reveal a scattered landscape of 70 variant 6G ecosystem concepts from 140 selected papers and emphasize the crucial role of ecosystem-level business innovation for a sustainable 6G ecosystem. Furthermore, this study provides foundational knowledge for stakeholders to strategically navigate this complex ecosystem and make corporate foresight decisions in the forthcoming 6G era, meanwhile offering insights for policymakers to foster collaboration and implement 6G standardization.

Keywords: 6G ecosystem · conceptual analysis · literature review

1 Introduction

Research on the sixth-generation wireless communication technology (6G) ecosystem has increased substantially over the past five years, capturing the interest of both academics and industrial [29]. This heightened attention was generated from ubiquitous anticipation that 6G will serve as a pivotal game changer [11] when compared to its predecessors. Although 6G technologies and standardization are still in their developmental stages and are expected to be commercialized in 2030 [11], they have attracted huge attention and interest due to the unprecedented opportunities they offer for ecosystem-level business innovation. Such innovation relies on corporate foresight decision making which necessitates collaboration across multi-perspective, multi-disciplinary, and multi-stakeholders [2]. In 2018, Finland launched a flagship program aiming at developing a complete 6G ecosystem through collaboration among academies, research organizations, industry and regulators [29,31]. This prospective research underscores the importance of analysing, discussing and fostering 6G ecosystem.

© The Author(s), under exclusive license to Springer Nature Switzerland AG 2025
D. Petrik et al. (Eds.): ICDPM 2024, LNBIP 528, pp. 75–90, 2025.
https://doi.org/10.1007/978-3-031-71515-0_6

Unfortunately, despite the extensive attention directed towards the 6G ecosystem and its concept variants, audiences often struggle to understand its antecedents and precisely grasp the essence of it, due to a lack of concept-level research work. Many digital ecosystems derived from 6G ecosystem research adopt "6G ecosystem" concept as a foundation without offering a clear definition within their studies. For instance, paper [7] discusses unmanned aerial vehicles within 6G ecosystem without a clear definition, and similarly, paper [33] explores digital service design in 6G ecosystem without explaining what 6G ecosystem is. Numerous instances of misusing the concept of "6G ecosystem" without well-defined risk relegating it to a potential zombie category [9]. To prevent the concept of "6G ecosystem" from becoming a zombie category [26, c.f.], it is imperative to undertake a comprehensive conceptual analysis during its formative and developmental stages, which essentially means now, before the launch of 6G.

In this paper, we review the current state of 6G ecosystem concept and propose a conceptual analysis framework for this emerging ecosystem through the following research question (RQ):

RQ: What are the related concepts and sub-concepts of 6G ecosystem, and how do they contribute to its antecedents and consequences?

When discussing the concept of 6G ecosystem, it transcends the mere definition of a phenomenon [51] which refers to the new generation of telecommunication appears; rather, it serves as a contextually bound tool for communication [57] among stakeholders in this 6G ecosystem. Our research does not seek to prescribe a singular correct interpretation of the 6G ecosystem or determine optimal usage scenarios. Instead, this conceptual-analytical paper aims to identify conceptual ambiguities with 6G ecosystem sub-concepts, clarify conceptual confusions related to 6G ecosystem related concepts, delve into the foundational knowledge of the 6G domain, and suggest practical implications for employing various 6G ecosystem concepts in specific scenarios.

Specifically, this conceptual analysis paper will:

(i) understand the emerging trends and dynamics of 6G ecosystem formation;
(ii) provide foundation knowledge for digital service design, business innovation, and corporate foresight decision-making in the forthcoming 6G era;
(iii) assist the stakeholders in positioning their roles in this complex and intricate 6G ecosystem;
(iv) offer valuable insights for policymakers to foster collaboration in the 6G ecosystem and implementation of 6G standardization.

The paper is structured as follows. Section 2 introduces the proposed conceptual analysis research approach. In the following Sect. 3, a comprehensive review of the literature is performed to present the 70 types of 6G ecosystem related concepts from 140 selected papers. Section 4 analyses the components of 6G ecosystem, examining them from various angles including technologies, vision, stakeholders, and business models. The complete conceptual framework of 6G ecosystem is outlined and analyzed in Sect. 5. Finally, Sect. 6 concludes the findings, presents the implications, and points out the limitations of this research.

2   Methodology

This paper adopted the conceptual analysis research approach [46], to recognise, categorize and clarify the 6G ecosystem concept. Conceptual analysis assists us in achieving conceptual refinement by disambiguation of current terminology and identifying potentially significant conceptual differences [43]. It is a systematic study of concepts [43] proposed by Wilson in 1969 [57], originally widely used in nursing science. Our software engineering field borrowed many methods from other disciplines, including conceptual analysis, despite being relatively young. Based on Wilson [57], Rogers [48], and Walker & Avant's [56] conceptual analysis model, an eight-step conceptual analysis methodology is proposed, as shown in Fig. 1 and adopted in this paper. There are two key phases: components analysis and conceptual framework development. The first one aims at distinguishing, analysing, and representing diverse definitions and components of 6G ecosystem. In the conceptual framework phase, leveraging the identified definition and components of 6G ecosystem, we generated insights into antecedents, consequences, related concepts and sub-concepts of 6G ecosystem, providing a knowledge foundation for corporate foresight decision-making theory development, innovative digital service design, and 6G ecosystem management. The data supporting both phases was collected through a literature review conducted with rigorous and systematic principles.

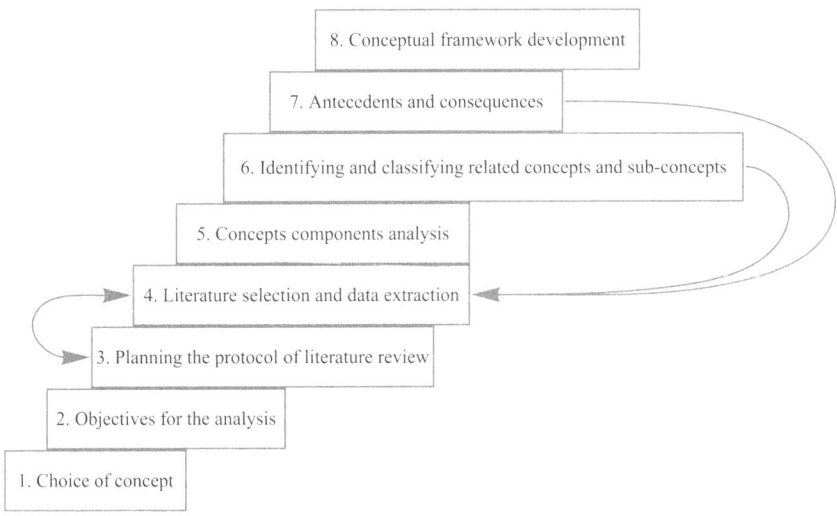

Fig. 1. Eight-step conceptual analysis methodology

3   Literature Review

To deeply understand the concept definition of the 6G ecosystem and its related concepts and sub-concepts, a literature review was conducted systematically. We followed Keele's guidelines for performing systematic literature reviews in software engineering [30] to conduct this review process.

The Scopus database was utilized as the source of data collection because it is known as the world's largest abstract and citation database of scientific literature [30,50]. The initial search used the term "6G ecosystem" within the title, keywords, and abstract fields, yielding a total of 247 papers. Subsequent exclusive steps involved the exclusion of duplicated, non-telecommunication contexts and conference proceedings which are not actual research papers, resulting in 180 articles. Within these papers, 140 papers were included in the final dataset because they focused on concepts related to 6G ecosystem. Others are not included because they just take 6G as one enabling technology for other ecosystems non-related to 6G. Figure 2 illustrates the process of this literature review.

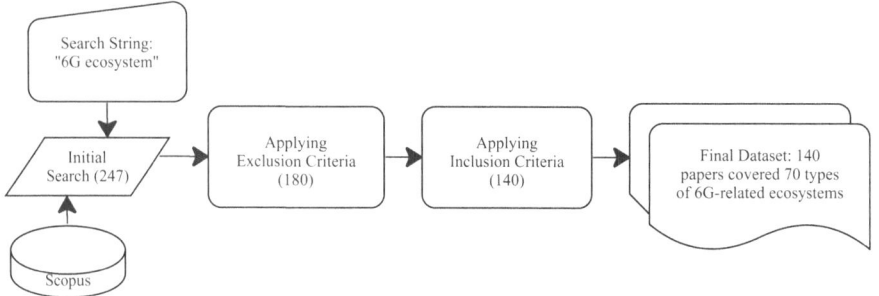

Fig. 2. Process of literature review

The final dataset addressed 70 distinct types of concepts related to 6G ecosystem across various dimensions, as depicted in Fig. 3. Some articles adopted more than one concept, resulting in a total of 154 instances that 6G ecosystem related concepts were mentioned. The most prominent one is the "6G ecosystem", mentioned in 41 papers. Other notable concept types include the "the fifth-generation wireless communication technology (5G) ecosystem" (mentioned 13 times), the "Internet of Things (IoT) ecosystem" (mentioned 7 times), and the "Micro/Nanotechnologies ecosystem" (mentioned 3 times). Some concepts look very similar, for example, "mobile communications ecosystem", "mobile ecosystem", "mobile network ecosystem", and "network ecosystem". However, we refrained from merging them to allow for further investigation into whether these concepts carry identical meanings.

The related concept of 6G ecosystem was first introduced in the paper titled *6Genesis Flagship Program: Building the Bridges Towards 6G-Enabled Wireless Smart Society and Ecosystem* in 2018 [29]. This seminal paper envisions the

Fig. 3. 70 distinct types of concepts related to 6G ecosystem identified from 140 papers

future of 6G by utilizing the concept of "wireless ecosystem". Since its inception, the annual publishing count of 6G ecosystem related concepts has increased significantly, particularly evident from 2020 to 2023, as illustrated by the blue line in Fig. 4. Similarly, there has been a steady increase in publications solely focusing on 6G ecosystem, but not reaching mainstream status. This literature review was conducted in February 2024, hence the limited data available for that year. It is anticipated that the data for 2024 will continue to grow as the year progresses.

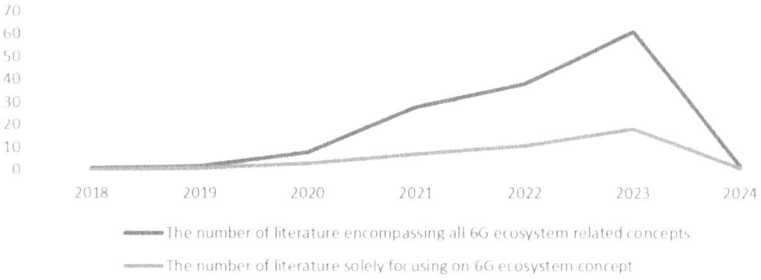

Fig. 4. Numbers of literature published between 2018 to 2024

4   Analysis of 6G Ecosystem Components

While reading the selected papers, we noticed that many articles directly used the concept 6G ecosystem without clarifying what it is. For instance, in paper [7], the authors discuss the highly reliable and harmonized integration of the unmanned aerial vehicle in the 6G ecosystem without providing a precise definition. Similarly, in another paper by Kovtun et al. [33], the authors proposed a mathematical apparatus that can be used at the design stage of client-oriented 4G, 5G, and, potentially, 6G ecosystems, yet they do not explicitly define what constitutes the 6G ecosystem. Moreover, in another selected paper by Moussaoui et al. [42], the authors interchangeably use five related concepts throughout their work: "mobile network ecosystem", "telecom ecosystem", "telecommunications ecosystem", "beyond 5G ecosystem", and "6G ecosystem". While these concepts appear to denote similar meanings, their exact definitions, clarifications, and differences are not provided within the text. Consequently, as readers, we encounter difficulty in comprehending the core concepts repeatedly mentioned in the paper and discerning how they differ from each other or the usage in other researcher's papers [27]. To understand the key concept 6G ecosystem while distinguishing it from various variants, we decompose 6G ecosystem as follows.

The 6G ecosystem comprises key components including technologies, vision, stakeholders, and business models. Among these, technologies serve as the fundamental building blocks of most digital ecosystems. While 6G telecommunication technology [69] is surely the foundation of 6G ecosystem but it is just one piece of the puzzle. 6G has been widely recognized as a convergence of emerging technological trends [37], encompassing technical innovations such as Software-defined Networking(SDN) [4,40,54,70], Artificial Intelligence (AI) [4,54,70], blockchain [1,28,62], IoT [35], Digital Twin [4,16], Cutting-edge Mobile Computing [18], and more. Notably, wireless communication technology, SDN, and AI stand out as the core technologies driving advancements within the 6G ecosystem [61]. As Martin mentioned in the paper [37], the SDN 6G is taking network softwarization to an unprecedented level. This evolution has led to the emergence of the concept "6G software ecosystem" [61]. 6G is an AI-driven ecosystem [18,54,70,71], and AI is expected to deliver breakthroughs and improvements in terms of massive data management and security [53]. The role of blockchain in 6G ecosystem [28] enhances the network reliability and effectiveness [1] as well as provides opportunities for business model transformations [62].

Bhat and Alqahtani [11] highlight the crux of 6G visions by aligning them with United Nation's Sustainability Development Goals (SDGs) for 2030. It is imperative to conceive and envision 6G as an ultimate ecosystem of communication technology solutions [29,44,60]. This entails adopting a more comprehensive, sustainable, multi-perspective, multi-disciplinary and multi-stakeholder approach [2]. Understanding how to identify and harmonize business, regulation, and technology needs forms the basis for bringing stakeholders together to solve long-term sustainability challenges [38]. Gathering relevant stakeholders [66] to envision a preferred sustainable future 6G ecosystem is crucial for long-term ecosystem viability.

The 6G era needs a transformation in how data is collected, stored, shared, analyzed, and acted upon [66]. This evolution introduces novel stakeholders into 6G ecosystem. Besides traditional stakeholders ranging from equipment manufacturers to application developers [11], 6G ecosystem opens the market for new stakeholders like micro-operators, edge cloud operators and resource brokers [62,63], and any stakeholder can act as a service provide [38]. In addition to openness, trustworthiness stands as another proclaimed principle within the 6G multi-player ecosystem [22,49]. This is underscored by the intricate interdependence of regulatory, business, and technical perspectives within this complex multi-stakeholder environment [38]. All stakeholders contribute their resources to the common pool and collaborate through shared business models to mutually benefit from 6G ecosystem [66].

In the 6G context, the essence of the ecosystem-focused business model lies in promoting value co-creation and co-capture to enhance the collective value of the ecosystem, which in turn boosts the value shared by all stakeholders within the ecosystem instead of a focal one [62]. More vertical [38] and collaborative business models [66] emerge through new venues for organizing value processes and expanding the range of business opportunities [67]. In the future 6G ecosystem, stakeholders are poised to adopt increasingly platform-based ecosystem business models [63]. A trend is emerging wherein the evolution of 5G business models transforms from innovation platform-based towards novel transaction platform-based ecosystem models in the realm of 6G [63].

5   Conceptual Framework of 6G Ecosystem

Figure 5 outlines the major building blocks of the conceptual analysis framework, which is alternatively regarded as a concept map or concept diagram. Based on the four components of 6G ecosystem concept in Sect. 4 as a foundation, this framework includes antecedents and consequences of 6G ecosystem and presents its related concepts as well as sub-concepts. By exploring the antecedents and consequences of the 6G ecosystem, we aim to understand how tangible and sustainable this concept is. While identifying related concepts and sub-concepts from the 70 concepts in Fig. 3 helps us know the context and scenario for using them.

5.1   Antecedents of 6G Ecosystem

Antecedents are the events that must happen before the occurrence of the 6G ecosystem concept [56]. In the 5G and generations before, telecommunication technologies are the key antecedents when a new-generation telecommunication ecosystem appears. 6G ecosystem would continue the trend of the previous generation, incorporating new services alongside the integration of emerging technologies [47]. But unlike 6G's predecessors, which were primarily designed to enhance network performance in terms of greater bandwidth, lower latency, and improved reliability, 6G ecosystem is redefined [1] and envisioned as a platform

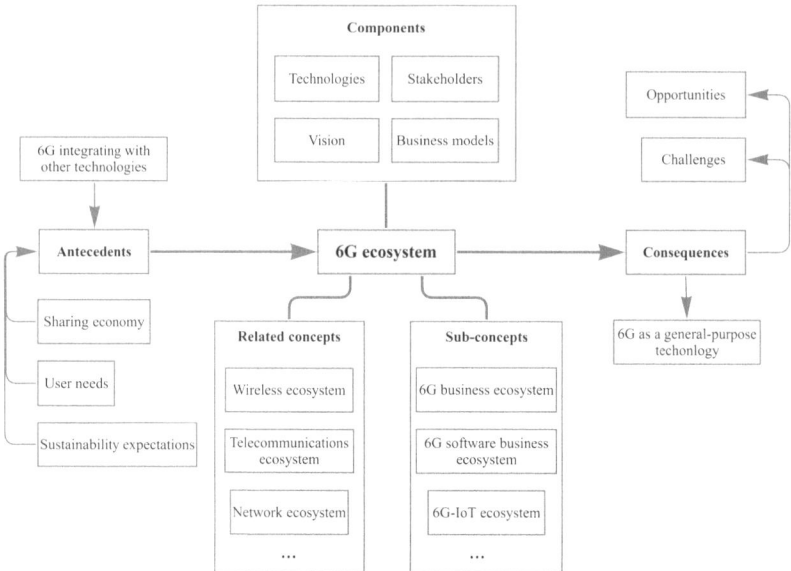

Fig. 5. Conceptual analysis framework of 6G ecosystem

fostering innovations across various domains, including computing, AI, connectivity and sensors, virtualization, and more [31]. The evolution from 5G towards 6G entails the establishment of a transaction ecosystem platform, essentially creating a marketplace for all the virtualized 6G network resources [63].

Beyond advanced technologies, the antecedents of the 6G ecosystem encompass significant social and business elements, notably the sharing economy, user needs, and sustainability expectations. The 6G ecosystem is inherent value-sharing oriented, with the openness of business models in the sharing economy [66] serving as a key antecedent [63]. Sharing refers to spectrum sharing supported by spectrum access models with different levels of rights [38], network infrastructure sharing, and deployment of equitable cost and revenue sharing models [39]. When contemplating user needs within 6G ecosystem, it is crucial to encompass all entities that communicate and derive benefits from it, rather than solely focusing on human beings, since 6G tightly integrates human, physical, and digital worlds [11]. At the social systemic level, 6G ecosystem needs to align sustainability vision with stable regulations and implement anticipatory measures that foster both open innovation and sustainability [3].

5.2 Related Concepts of 6G Ecosystem

From the literature review data abstraction process, a word cloud Fig. 3 was generated and 18 related concepts were identified from 70 distinct types of 6G ecosystem. Within these related concepts, 6 of them appeared in more than one paper: "wireless ecosystem", "telecommunications ecosystem", "network ecosystem", "future wireless ecosystem", "mobile communications ecosystem", and "wireless telecommunication ecosystem ".

Wireless ecosystem is envisioned to mitigate the impediments of previous wireless generations and improve service availability, continuity, ubiquity and scalability [14]. 6G wireless ecosystem aims to revolutionize communication by leveraging satellite-terrestrial [6,8] integrated networks to deliver advanced services. With an expected very-high wireless device density [29] and as subscribers increase accordingly, supporting complex and time-sensitive tasks are key challenge for a high-performance wireless ecosystem [14]. Therefore, non-terrestrial Networks within 6G wireless ecosystem are essential to guarantee service availability, continuity, ubiquity, and scalability [6]. Moreover, ensuring dependable wireless communication requires methods that focus on building robust connections using parallel designs across both hardware and software components [29], which is related to another sub-concept of 6G ecosystem: "6G software business ecosystem".

Telecommunications ecosystem also regards the space industry and satellite network as a new groundbreaking opportunity, similar to the visions outlined within "wireless ecosystem" [68]. Moussaoui et al. conducted a survey study on the telecoms business ecosystem by analysing new stakeholders and emerging business models within this domain [41,42]. However, they mostly use the concept of "telecommunications ecosystem", "telecoms ecosystem", and "telecom ecosystem" instead of consistently and coherently using a more precise concept of "business ecosystem" throughout the entire paper.

Network ecosystem, alongside "wireless ecosystem" and "telecommunications ecosystem", emphasizes the importance of achieving comprehensive coverage across the air, space, sea and land domains [10,36]. However, the network ecosystem surpasses mere coverage by seamlessly integrating with AI, IoT, and blockchain technologies to enhance connectivity and functionality across diverse environments [36]. Additionally, within the diversified landscape of the 6G network ecosystem, blockchain technology is leveraged to meet the increasing demand for more flexible and efficient service provisioning [17].

"Future wireless ecosystem", "mobile communications ecosystem", and "wireless telecommunication ecosystem " are sub-concepts of wireless ecosystem and telecommunications ecosystem. Future wireless ecosystem is commonly used in discussions revolving around the advancement of wireless communication technologies and their applications. It involves topics such as antenna and array technologies [24], as well as topology search algorithms in ultra-dense networks [20]. 6G mobile communications ecosystem represents the evolving infrastructure and technologies aimed at providing global high-quality mobile broadband connectivity while exploring space-based coverage [32]. In Uusitalo et al.'s paper [55], the concept "6G mobile communications ecosystem" is employed alongside the "6G ecosystem" to denote a broader framework encompassing the 6G vision, technologies and standards, and challenges such as sustainability and trustworthiness with the ecosystem. In the realm of the "wireless telecommunication ecosystem", publications such as [59] and [52] explore the evolutionary trajectory of wireless communication technologies and infrastructure, focusing on radio access network components.

5.3   Sub-concepts of 6G Ecosystem

Six sub-concepts were identified from 70 concepts, "6G business ecosystem", "6G software business ecosystem", "6G industrial digital twins ecosystem", "6G IoE-Edge Intelligence ecosystem", "6G-enabled edge cloud ecosystem", and "6G-IoT ecosystem". The first two sub-concepts introduce a business perspective to the overarching 6G ecosystem, while "6G-IoT ecosystem" stands out as the most frequently discussed sub-concept. The remaining three sub-concepts represent two specific use case scenarios of 6G ecosystem, which are industrial massive twinning [25], and hybrid edge-cloud [21,45].

The business perspective consistently plays a crucial role in understanding the opportunities presented a new technology could provide [38]. Incorporating the term "business" within the context of 6G ecosystem emphasizes the stakeholders' roles, relationships, opportunities, and challenges in this emerging landscape [61,64]. According to experience from previous generations of wireless technology, it takes approximately 10 to 15 years from early academic research to full industrialization and commercialization [61]. Therefore, few papers currently integrate the term "business" into the discussion of the 6G ecosystem, but as 6G matures, more research on this is expected to emerge.

The increasing data volumes pose considerable bottlenecks for 6G-IoT network, which limits control, flexibility, interoperability [12], and energy efficiency performance [5,35]. Therefore, 6G-IoT ecosystem is envisioned to become automated, featuring self-configuring and self-healing capabilities, reducing the necessity for manual intervention in management and network orchestration services [12]. Besides autonomous [69], achieving ultra-low-power and optimizing energy usage are also crucial for 6G-IoT ecosystem [5,15].

5.4   Consequences of 6G Ecosystem

The consequences of 6G ecosystem refer to the outcomes and end-points that manifest as a result of various antecedents [58] and the concept analysis process. These consequences encompass both the positive and negative impacts stemming from 6G ecosystem development, affecting stakeholders across different domains. It includes opportunities particularly in fostering business innovation, as challenges arise from the convergence of technologies and the need to establish a sustainable ecosystem. As an expected long-term consequence, a sustainable 6G ecosystem has the potential to transform 6G into a general-purpose technology, benefiting the whole society.

As a decentralized ecosystem [62], the traditional business models and ecosystem roles will be changed to an open market for new stakeholders. Instead of previous business models driven by focal firms, 6G ecosystem proposes a novel decentralized marketplace and provides opportunities for stakeholders to establish and participate in the supply chain of virtualized network resources [63,65,67]. The value needs to be co-created and co-captured and the stakeholders need to explore their competitive advantages in the 6G ecosystem [66].

Digital convergence and multi-stakeholders 6G ecosystems are creating a complex strategic environment, offering incomparable and distinct opportunities as well as emerging issues [38]. Challenges mainly come from the integration of various aforementioned enabling technologies including AI, blockchain [62], IoT etc. as well as wireless local area networks in a 6G ecosystem [19]. Also, ensuring the sustainability of a heterogeneous 6G ecosystem poses another significant challenge, as does establishing regulations that effectively govern the use of data and connectivity platforms within this ecosystem.

There has been considerable contemplation towards positioning 6G as the ultimate ecosystem of communication technology solutions [29,44,60]. This perspective suggests an expectation of a long lifespan for 6G, characterized by ongoing innovation within its ecosystem, which aligns with the characteristics of general-purpose technology [13,23,34,71]. The aspiration is for 6G to evolve into a pervasive general-purpose technology, as highlighted in the work by Yrjölä et al. [67]. Efforts towards this future-oriented 6G scenario [66] involve collaborative research, harmonized standardization, and anticipatory regulation [67].

6 Conclusions

The scattered nature of variant 6G ecosystem concepts is unsurprising given its status as an emerging ecosystem [3] under development, lacking prior conceptual analysis work. Notably, the trajectory of 6G suggests a convergence of technologies [37], drawing input from researchers across disciplinary technical backgrounds who bring their domain-specific terminologies to 6G ecosystem. Examples include concepts like "wireless ecosystem" [6,8,14,29], "telecommunications ecosystem" [41,42,68], "network ecosystem" [10,17,36]. However, it is crucial to acknowledge instances where these concepts have already been misused, with some papers referring to several different concepts of 6G ecosystem in one single paper without definition or clarification [33,42]. It poses the risk of the 6G ecosystem being a zombie category, which indicates that researchers have been shaking and renewing [26] this novel ecosystem. Rather than aiming to standardise definitions or correct such misuses, our study preserved all raw data, conducted analyses based on them, and fostered discussion around selecting an appropriate ecosystem type for specific contexts. This work presents an accurate portrayal of the state of the 6G ecosystem concept, intending to curb further misuse and prevent the emergence of a "zombie ecosystem".

The research question was addressed and deliberated upon during the conceptual analysis process, which was underpinned by the identification of 70 distinct concepts related to 6G ecosystem from a pool of 140 selected papers via literature review, as shown in Fig. 2. Among these, Sect. 5.2 uncovered 18 related concepts, with 6 of them being recurrently adopted in more than one paper: "wireless ecosystem", "telecommunications ecosystem", "network ecosystem", "future wireless ecosystem", "mobile communications ecosystem", and "wireless telecommunication ecosystem". Additionally, 6 sub-concepts emerge, including "6G business ecosystem", "6G software business ecosystem", "6G industrial digital twins ecosystem", "6G IoE-Edge Intelligence ecosystem", "6G-enabled edge cloud ecosystem", and "6G-IoT ecosystem", with two of them involve the software business domain. These concepts were thoroughly analysed and discussed within this paper, revealing their antecedents that were predominantly influenced by 6G and its enabling technologies. Moreover, our study highlights the significance of business-driven antecedents and suggests the potential for a sustainable 6G ecosystem to evolve into a general-purpose technology, driven by business innovation, as a long-term consequence.

6.1   Implications

Our research is a pioneering research work in analysing the concept of 6G ecosystem and the foundational knowledge of 6G ecosystem management. Undertaking such conceptual-level research at the inception of a new ecosystem is of significant importance. It allows us to transcend the conventional focus solely on technical innovation and instead emphasizes the crucial role of business factors. Recognizing that ecosystem-level business innovation is paramount, both for antecedents and consequences of 6G ecosystem, becomes imperative. Specifically, our study highlights the pivotal role of business model openness in the sharing economy environment, which facilitates the emergence of 6G ecosystem and business strategic decision-making. Moreover, we emphasize the transformative potential of stakeholders' roles in this novel decentralized ecosystem.

The literature review process systematically retrospects the emerging trends of 6G and its related ecosystems. The resulting framework can be utilized as foundational knowledge for stakeholders' strategic deployment in the developing 6G ecosystem. It empowers forthcoming stakeholders to strategically position their roles and benefit from this complex and intricate ecosystem. Especially the policymakers, who are also stakeholders in 6G ecosystem, will gain valuable insights from this conceptual analysis, and better know how to navigate the challenge issues.

6.2   Limitations and Future Work

This study conducts the conceptual analysis research work through theoretical material, i.e. white literature. Empiricists may think more empirical evidence needs to be considered while analysing concepts. We may consider the empirical material, like data from case studies or workshops, in future work. Besides, grey literature may also be considered in the literature review process to ensure more comprehensive coverage of the topic. Feedback and comments from 6G industrial participators and organisations will help this conceptual analysis framework improve.

Acknowledgements. This research was funded by the Business Finland project 6G Bridge - 6G software for extremely distributed and heterogeneous massive networks of connected devices (8516/31/2022).

References

1. Ahmed, S., Kumar, V., Singh, K., Singh, A., Muthukumaran, V., Gupta, D.: 6G enabled federated learning for secure IoMT resource recommendation and propagation analysis. IEEE Internet Things J. (2023)
2. Ahokangas, P., Matinmikko-Blue, M., Yrjölä, S.: Envisioning a future-proof global 6g from business, regulation, and technology perspectives. IEEE Commun. Mag. **61**(2), 72–78 (2022)
3. Ahokangas, P., Yrjölä, S., Matinmikko-Blue, M., Seppänen, V., Koivumäki, T.: Antecedents of future 6G mobile ecosystems. In: 2020 2nd 6G Wireless Summit (6G SUMMIT), pp. 1–5. IEEE (2020)
4. Alja'Afreh, M., Karime, A., Alouneh, S., El Saddik, A.: A detailed analysis of qualitative and quantitative factors in realization of 6g communication. In: 2022 9th International Conference on Internet of Things: Systems, Management and Security (IOTSMS), pp. 1–10. IEEE (2022)
5. Ansere, J.A., Kamal, M., Khan, I.A., Aman, M.N.: Dynamic resource optimization for energy-efficient 6G-IoT ecosystems. Sensors **23**(10), 4711 (2023)
6. Araniti, G., Iera, A., Pizzi, S., Rinaldi, F.: Toward 6g non-terrestrial networks. IEEE Network **36**(1), 113–120 (2021)
7. Azari, M., Solanki, S., Chatzinotas, S., Bennis, M.: THZ-empowered UAVs in 6G: opportunities, challenges, and trade-offs. IEEE Trans. Wirel. Commun. (2023)
8. Azari, M., et al.: Evolution of non-terrestrial networks from 5G to 6G: a survey. IEEE Commun. Surv. Tutor. (2023)
9. Beck, U.: Interview with ulrich beck. J. Consum. Cult. **1**(2), 261–277 (2001)
10. Beshley, M., Klymash, M., Scherm, I., Beshley, H., Shkoropad, Y.: Emerging network technologies for digital transformation: 5G/6G, IoT, SDN/IBN, cloud computing, and blockchain. In: Klymash, M., Luntovskyy, A., Beshley, M., Melnyk, I., Schill, A. (eds.) IEEE International Conference on Advanced Trends in Radioelectronics, Telecommunications and Computer Engineering, pp. 1–20. Springer, Cham (2022). https://doi.org/10.1007/978-3-031-24963-1_1
11. Bhat, J., Alqahtani, S.: 6G ecosystem: current status and future perspective. IEEE Commun. Stand. Mag. (2023)
12. Bhattacharya, P., Mukherjee, A., Tanwar, S., Pricop, E.: Zero-load: a zero touch network based router management scheme underlying 6G-IoT ecosystems. In: 2023 15th International Conference on Electronics, Computers and Artificial Intelligence (ECAI), pp. 1–7. IEEE (2023)
13. Bresnahan, T.F., Trajtenberg, M.: General purpose technologies 'engines of growth'? J. Econom. **65**(1), 83–108 (1995)
14. Cao, X., et al.: Edge-assisted multi-layer offloading optimization of leo satellite-terrestrial integrated networks. IEEE J. Sel. Areas Commun. **41**(2), 381–398 (2022)
15. Chaudhri, S.N., Rajput, N.S., Alsamhi, S.H., Shvetsov, A.V., Almalki, F.A.: Zero-padding and spatial augmentation-based gas sensor node optimization approach in resource-constrained 6G-IoT paradigm. Sensors **22**(8), 3039 (2022)
16. Chavhan, S., et al.: Shift to 6G: exploration on trends, vision, requirements, technologies, research, and standardization efforts. Sustainable Energy Technol. Assess. **54**, 102666 (2022)

17. Chen, S., Lin, Y., Zhang, R., Liu, Y.: Blockchain-based distributed service registry and discovery in 6G core network. In: 2023 8th International Conference on Computer and Communication Systems (ICCCS), pp. 714–718. IEEE (2023)

18. Demanboro, A.C., Bianchini, D., Iano, Y., de Oliveira, G.G., Vaz, G.C.: 6G networks: an innovative approach, but with many challenges and paradigms, in the development of platforms and services in the near future. In: Brazilian Technology Symposium, pp. 172–187. Springer, Cham (2021). https://doi.org/10.1007/978-3-031-04435-9_17

19. Edirisinghe, S., Galagedarage, O., Dias, I., Ranaweera, C.: Recent development of emerging indoor wireless networks towards 6G. IEEE Wirel. Commun. (2023)

20. Fokin, G., Koucheryavy, A.: Algorithm for topology search using dilution of precision criterion in ultra-dense network positioning service area. Mathematics **11**(10), 2227 (2023)

21. Garg, S., Kaur, K., Aujla, G.S., Kaddoum, G., Garigipati, P., Guizani, M.: Trusted explainable AI for 6G-enabled edge cloud ecosystem. IEEE Wirel. Commun. **30**(3), 163–170 (2023)

22. Garzon, S., Yildiz, H., Kupper, A.: Towards decentralized identity management in multi-stakeholder 6G networks. IEEE Commun. Mag. (2023)

23. Goldfarb, A., Taska, B., Teodoridis, F.: Could machine learning be a general purpose technology? A comparison of emerging technologies using data from online job postings. Res. Policy **52**(1), 104653 (2023)

24. Guo, Y.J., Ziolkowski, R.W.: Antenna and Array Technologies for Future Wireless Ecosystems. Wiley, Hoboken (2022)

25. Han, B., et al.: Digital twins for industry 4.0 in the 6G era. IEEE Open J. Veh. Technol. (2023)

26. Hyrynsalmi, S., Hyrynsalmi, S.M.: Ecosystem: a zombie category? In: 2019 IEEE International Conference on Engineering, Technology and Innovation (ICE/ITMC), pp. 1–8. IEEE (2019)

27. Kakkuri-Knuuttila, M.: Hypoteesien testaus. teoksessa kakkuri-knuuttila ml.(toim): Argumentti ja kritiikki. lukemisen, keskustelu ja vaikuttamisen taidot (1998)

28. Kalla, A., de Alwis, C., Porambage, P., Gür, G., Liyanage, M.: A survey on the use of blockchain for future 6G: technical aspects, use cases, challenges and research directions. IEEE Trans. Network Serv. Manag. (2023)

29. Katz, M., Matinmikko-Blue, M., Latva-Aho, M.: 6genesis flagship program: building the bridges towards 6G-enabled wireless smart society and ecosystem. In: 2018 IEEE 10th Latin-American Conference on Communications (LATINCOM), pp. 1–9. IEEE (2018)

30. Keele, S., et al.: Guidelines for performing systematic literature reviews in software engineering (2007)

31. Khanh, Q., Chehri, A., Quy, N., Han, N., Ban, N.: Innovative trends in the 6G era: a comprehensive survey of architecture, applications, technologies, and challenges. IEEE Access **11**, 39824–39844 (2023)

32. Kharlan, A., Biktimirov, S., Ivanov, A.: A business case analysis for satellite backhaul network in 5G/6G mobile networks. In: Proceedings of the International Astronautical Congress, IAC (2020)

33. Kovtun, V., Izonin, I., Gregus, M.: Formalization of the metric of parameters for quality evaluation of the subject-system interaction session in the 5G-IoT ecosystem. Int. J. Open Inf. Technol. (2023)

34. Liao, H., Wang, B., Li, B., Weyman-Jones, T.: ICT as a general-purpose technology: the productivity of ICT in the united states revisited. Inf. Econ. Policy **36**, 10–25 (2016)
35. Lin, W., Ziolkowski, R.: High performance electrically small huygens rectennas enable wirelessly powered internet of things sensing applications: a review. IEEE Antennas Wirel. Propag. Lett. (2023)
36. Lu, Y., Ning, X.: A vision of 6G–5G's successor. J. Manag. Anal. **7**(3), 301–320 (2020)
37. Maier, M.: Toward 6G: a new era of convergence. In: Optical Fiber Communication Conference, pp. F4H–1. Optica Publishing Group (2021)
38. Matinmikko-Blue, M., Yrjölä, S., Ahokangas, P.: Moving from 5G in verticals to sustainable 6G: business, regulatory and technical research prospects. Sustainability **15**(1), 135 (2023)
39. Matinmikko-Blue, M., et al.: White paper on 6G drivers and the un SDGS. arXiv preprint arXiv:2004.14695 (2020)
40. Matinmikko-Blue, M., Yrjölä, S., Ahokangas, P.: Moving from 5G in verticals to sustainable 6G: business, regulatory and technical research prospects. In: Caso, G., De Nardis, L., Gavrilovska, L. (eds.) CrownCom 2020. LNICST, vol. 374, pp. 176–191. Springer, Cham (2021). https://doi.org/10.1007/978-3-030-73423-7_13
41. Moussaoui, M., Bertin, E., Crespi, N.: Telecom business models for beyond 5g and 6g networks: towards disaggregation? In: 2022 1st International Conference on 6G Networking (6GNet), pp. 1–8. IEEE (2022)
42. Moussaoui, M., Bertin, E., Crespi, N.: Divide and conquer: a business model agenda for beyond-5G and 6G. IEEE Commun. Mag. **61**(7), 82–88 (2023)
43. Olsthoorn, J.: Conceptual analysis. In: Methods in Analytical Political Theory, pp. 153–191 (2017)
44. Peltonen, E., Leppänen, T., Lovén, L.: Edgeai: edge-native distributed platform for artificial intelligence. In: Proceedings of the 1st 6G Wireless Summit, Levi, Finland, pp. 24–26 (2019)
45. Picano, B., Fantacci, R.: A channel-aware FL approach for virtual machine placement in 6G edge intelligent ecosystems. ACM Trans. Internet Things **4**(2), 1–20 (2023)
46. Puusa, A.: Käsiteanalyysi tutkimusmenetelmänä. Premissi **4**(2008), 36–43 (2008)
47. Rico-Palomo, J., Galeano-Brajones, J., Cortes-Polo, D., Valenzuela-Valdes, J., Carmona-Murillo, J.: Chained orchestrator algorithm for ran-slicing resource management: a contribution to ultra-reliable 6G communications. IEEE Access **10**, 113662–113677 (2023)
48. Rodgers, B.L.: Concepts, analysis and the development of nursing knowledge: the evolutionary cycle. J. Adv. Nurs. **14**(4), 330–335 (1989)
49. Rong, B.: 6G: the next horizon: from connected people and things to connected intelligence. IEEE Wirel. Commun. **28**(5), 8–8 (2021)
50. Schotten, M., Meester, W.J., Steiginga, S., Ross, C.A., et al.: A brief history of scopus: the world's largest abstract and citation database of scientific literature. In: Research Analytics, pp. 31–58. Auerbach Publications (2017)
51. Schwartz-Barcott, D.: An expansion and elaboration of the hybrid model of concept development. In: Concept Development in Nursing Foundations, Techniques, and Applications, pp. 129–159 (2000)
52. Secgin, S.: Evolution of Wireless Communication Ecosystems. Wiley, Hoboken (2023)

53. Telecom, S.: SKT publishes 6G white paper to present blueprint for future networks (2023). https://ee.cdnartwhere.eu/wp-content/uploads/2023/08/SKT6G-White-PaperEng-v1.0-web.pdf. Accessed 25 Feb 2024
54. Uusitalo, M.A., et al.: Hexa-x the European 6G flagship project. In: 2021 Joint European Conference on Networks and Communications & 6G Summit (EuCNC/6G Summit), pp. 580–585. IEEE (2021)
55. Uusitalo, M.A., et al.: 6G vision, value, use cases and technologies from European 6G flagship project hexa-x. IEEE Access **9**, 160004–160020 (2021)
56. Walker, L.O., Avant, K.C., et al.: Strategies for Theory Construction in Nursing, vol. 4. Pearson/Prentice Hall, Upper Saddle River (2005)
57. Wilson, J.: Thinking with Concepts. Cambridge University Press, Cambridge (1970)
58. Windle, G.: What is resilience? A review and concept analysis. Rev. Clin. Gerontol. **21**(2), 152–169 (2011)
59. Yamany, S.M.: The evolution of ran. Open RAN: The Definitive Guide, pp. 1–13 (2023)
60. Yang, H., Alphones, A., Xiong, Z., Niyato, D., Zhao, J., Wu, K.: Artificial-intelligence-enabled intelligent 6G networks. IEEE Network **34**(6), 272–280 (2020)
61. Yang, N.: Exploring the 6G software business ecosystem: a morphological analysis approach. Wirel. Commun. Mob. Comput. **2023**, 1–14 (2023)
62. Yrjola, S.: How could blockchain transform 6g towards open ecosystemic business models? IEEE Network (2023)
63. Yrjola, S., Matinmikko-Blue, M., Ahokangas, P.: How could 6G transform engineering platforms towards ecosystemic business models? IEEE Network (2023)
64. Yrjölä, S.: Legitimation of newness challenges and opportunities in the 6G era. In: 2023 IEEE 34th Annual International Symposium on Personal, Indoor and Mobile Radio Communications (PIMRC), pp. 1–6. IEEE (2023)
65. Yrjölä, S., et al.: Decentralized 6G business models. In: Proceedings of the 6G Wireless Summit, Levi, Finland, pp. 5–7 (2019)
66. Yrjölä, S., Ahokangas, P., Matinmikko-Blue, M.: Sustainability as a challenge and driver for novel ecosystemic 6G business scenarios. IEEE Network (2023)
67. Yrjölä, S., Matinmikko-Blue, M., Ahokangas, P.: Developing 6G visions with stakeholder analysis of 6G ecosystem. IEEE Network (2023)
68. Zaglauer, H.W., et al.: Integrated satellite access to 5G/6G systems-an overview of the 5G space infrastructure study (2023)
69. Zhang, Z., et al.: 6G wireless networks: vision, requirements, architecture, and key technologies. IEEE Network (2023)
70. Ziegler, V., Yrjola, S.: 6G indicators of value and performance. In: 2020 2nd 6G Wireless Summit (6G SUMMIT), pp. 1–5. IEEE (2020)
71. Ziegler, V., Yrjölä, S.: How to make 6g a general purpose technology: prerequisites and value creation paradigm shift. In: 2021 Joint European Conference on Networks and Communications & 6G Summit (EuCNC/6G Summit), pp. 586–591. IEEE (2021)

From Compliance Risk to Business Model - Cloud Sovereignty as a Door Opener for the EU Market

Philipp Hofer[(✉)] and Georg Herzwurm

University of Stuttgart, Keplerstr. 17, 70174 Stuttgart, Germany
{philipp.hofer,georg.herzwurm}@bwi.uni-stuttgart.de

Abstract. The increasing use of cloud services presents companies with new challenges in terms of compliance and data protection. The conflict between the US CLOUD Act and European data protection regulations such as the General Data Protection Regulation (GDPR) leads to considerable uncertainties and risks. In this context, the concept of cloud sovereignty is becoming increasingly important. This paper uses a secondary data analysis to examine how European cloud providers can leverage the challenges of cloud sovereignty to differentiate themselves in the market and develop new business models. The study reveals that Europe's regulatory framework can drive innovation and competitive advantage. By developing trustworthy and legally compliant cloud solutions, European providers can meet the demand for secure and sovereign cloud services and position themselves as an alternative to large US providers, thereby tapping into significant market potential.

Keywords: Cloud Computing · Digital Sovereignty · GDPR · US CLOUD Act

1 Introduction

Advancing digitalization and the associated increase in the use of cloud services present companies with new challenges in the area of data security and data protection. In particular, the conflict between the US CLOUD Act and European data protection regulations, such as the General Data Protection Regulation (GDPR), has led to increased uncertainty in the use of cloud services [1].

The US CLOUD Act enables US authorities to access data processed by US companies under certain conditions, regardless of where this data is stored [2]. This is contrary to European data protection regulations, which provide for a high level of protection of personal data and only allow data to be transferred to third countries under strict conditions [3].

In this area of conflict, the concept of cloud sovereignty is becoming increasingly important. Cloud sovereignty refers to the ability of companies and organizations to retain control over their data in the cloud and ensure compliance with data protection regulations and compliance requirements [4].

The aim of this short paper is to show that cloud sovereignty not only reduces compliance risk, but can also be an opportunity for European cloud providers. By developing

D. Petrik et al. (Eds.): ICDPM 2024, LNBIP 528, pp. 91–97, 2025.
https://doi.org/10.1007/978-3-031-71515-0_7

trustworthy and legally compliant cloud solutions, European providers can differentiate themselves from the competition and benefit from the strict European data protection regulations.

This work will first examine the regulatory framework and the resulting challenges for cloud providers. It will then present approaches for trustworthy cloud infrastructures and analyze the business potential for European providers. Finally, the most important findings are summarized and an outlook on the future development of the cloud market in Europe is given.

2   Regulatory Framework

2.1   Core Requirements of the US CLOUD Act Regarding Data Transfer

The US CLOUD Act (Clarifying Lawful Overseas Use of Data Act) was passed in the USA in 2018 and grants US authorities the power to compel US-based technology companies, via warrant or subpoena, to provide requested data stored on their servers, regardless of whether the data is stored within the United States or on foreign soil [2].

The law raises concerns about the legal certainty and privacy of data stored with US cloud service providers. This criminal law scope and the extent of the US CLOUD Act is in conflict with EU data protection regulations [5].

2.2   EU Regulations GDPR and Data Act with Compliance Obligations

With the General Data Protection Regulation (GDPR) and the Data Act, the European Union has introduced strict regulations for the protection of personal data. The GDPR has been in force since May 2018 and stipulates that personal data may only be processed under certain conditions and with the consent of the data subject [3].

Companies must take appropriate technical and organizational measures to ensure data security [6]. The Data Act, which came into force on December 13, 2023, aims to regulate access to and use of data and improve data portability [7].

2.3   Potential Conflicts and Risks for US Cloud Providers

The conflict between the US CLOUD Act and European data protection regulations presents significant risks for both EU cloud users and US cloud providers operating in Europe [8].

The conflict was exacerbated by the decision of the European Court of Justice (ECJ) in the "Schrems II" case in July 2020, in which the ECJ declared the EU-US Privacy Shield agreement invalid [9]. The agreement had previously regulated the transfer of data between the EU and the US and offered US companies the opportunity to declare their compliance with data protection regulations through self-certification.

On July 20, 2023, the so-called EU-US Privacy Framework entered into force as a successor agreement, which is intended to regulate data transfers between the EU and the USA in a new way [10]. However, there are considerable doubts as to whether the Privacy Framework meets the requirements of the ECJ. Experts assume that the ECJ will also overturn the Privacy Framework as it does not provide sufficient guarantees for the protection of personal data [11].

For users of US cloud providers, this means that they cannot rely on the Privacy Framework and continue to be confronted with legal uncertainties.

3   Approaches for Trustworthy Cloud Infrastructures

3.1   Concepts for Sovereign Cloud Infrastructures

Several initiatives and concepts have been developed in Europe to meet the challenges in the area of cloud sovereignty. GAIA-X is an European project that aims to create a trustworthy and sovereign digital infrastructure for Europe. The aim is to anchor European values such as data protection, transparency and interoperability in the cloud [12].

The Sovereign Cloud Stack (SCS) is an open source solution that makes it possible to build a sovereign cloud infrastructure that meets data protection, security and compliance requirements [13]. Cloud-based data trustees can act as independent entities to ensure compliance with data protection regulations and data sovereignty [14].

Various providers of trustworthy cloud services have established themselves in Europe. With its Open Telekom Cloud, Deutsche Telekom offers a sovereign cloud platform based on European values and standards [15]. The French OVHcloud positions itself as an European alternative provider to the large US cloud providers and places particular emphasis on data protection and data sovereignty [16].

One example of an European provider that offers open source software for cloud environments is Nextcloud. The company offers a collaboration platform that enables companies to store and manage their data in their own cloud [17].

3.2   Technical Basics: Encryption and Open Source Software

Trustworthy cloud infrastructures are based on various technical foundations. End-to-end encryption can ensure that data is protected both during transmission and storage [18]. Open source software and open standards play a key role in the development of trustworthy and sovereign cloud infrastructures in Europe. They enable interoperability, transparency, and the avoidance of vendor lock-ins, thereby strengthening digital sovereignty and independence from individual providers [8].

4   Business Potential for European Cloud Providers

4.1   Methodological Approach: Secondary Data Analysis and Literature Review

In order to determine the business potential for European cloud providers, a secondary data analysis is carried out. This involves evaluating existing market data, studies and scientific publications in order to gain relevant insights [19]. Secondary data analysis is particularly suitable for gaining a broad overview of the market and identifying trends [20].

The research comprised market data and a derivation of market potential for trustworthy cloud solutions based on this data. In particular, current market research data collected from 2023 onwards was sought in order to best reflect the latest developments.

4.2   Market Data on Growth Rates for Cloud Services in Europe

According to the latest IDC Worldwide Software and Public Cloud Services Spending Guide, global spending on public cloud services is expected to reach USD 1.35 trillion by 2027. Although annual spending growth is expected to decline slightly over the forecast period 2023–2027, the market is forecast to grow at a compound annual growth rate (CAGR) of 19.9%.

The United States is projected to be the largest geographic market for public cloud services, with projected spending of USD 697 billion in 2027. Western Europe is expected to be the second largest market in 2027, with investments of USD 273 billion, as illustrated in Fig. 1 [21].

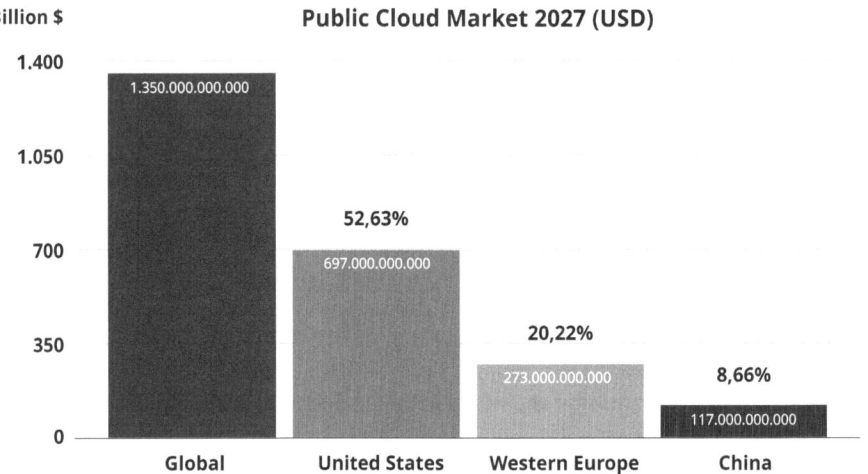

Fig. 1. Forecasted Spending for Global Public Cloud Market in 2027.

A study by Research and Markets predicts that the European cloud infrastructure services market is expected to grow at a CAGR of 19.8% during the forecast period 2023–2028 [22]. The rising demand for scalable and cost-efficient IT solutions and the increasing acceptance of cloud-native technologies are driving the growth of the market. In addition, digital transformation initiatives in various industries are accelerating the introduction of cloud services in Europe.

Globally, public cloud services are anticipated to experience a 19.1% growth in current US dollars in 2024. Companies continue to accelerate their adoption of cloud services, resulting in a compound annual growth rate of 19.3% over a five-year period according to Gartner Research [23].

This robust growth market, which, as evidenced by multiple studies, is approaching 20% annually, offers European cloud providers a significant business opportunity.

4.3   Forecasts and Estimates of Market Potential

Various studies have looked at the market potential for trustworthy and sovereign cloud services in Europe. A study on the strategic importance of cloud services for the digital sovereignty of SMEs (small and medium-sized businesses) showed potential for European solutions, especially if they can address the requirements for data protection, interoperability and digital sovereignty [24].

In some European countries, national providers such as Deutsche Telekom have so far been able to maintain a certain market share. This indicates a potential for locally anchored cloud services. The GAIA-X project is still in its initial phase, so its concrete effects are still unclear.

Another study by PwC, which conducted a survey in 20 countries in the EMEA region (Europe, Middle East, and Africa) with over 2,200 business and technology executives, found that 54% of EMEA organizations surveyed have already adopted cloud in many or all areas of their business and 73% of organizations plan to move their entire operations to the cloud within the next 2 years [25]. These forecasts highlight the considerable market potential for providers with trustworthy and sovereign cloud solutions.

4.4   Opportunity for Providers with Trustworthy Sovereign Cloud Solutions

The secondary data analysis shows that providers with trustworthy and sovereign cloud solutions have particularly good growth opportunities in Europe. By meeting European data protection and compliance requirements, these providers can meet the demand for secure and legally compliant cloud services to reduce user concerns about regulations [26].

A study by Capgemini shows that 71% of global companies will adopt cloud sovereignty to ensure compliance with regulations and standards of nation, state, and local government. Italy and Germany are particularly convinced, with 76% and 75% respectively [27].

The overwhelming presence of AWS, Microsoft Azure, and Google Cloud, which collectively holding a 67% global market share in Q4 2023 [28], can only be broken by European cloud providers by positioning themselves as a trustworthy alternative to the large US providers and thereby setting themselves apart.

5   Conclusion and Outlook

5.1   Regulation as a Driver for New Cloud Compliance Models

The previous chapters have shown that the regulatory framework, in particular the conflict between the US CLOUD Act and European data protection regulations, is driving the development of new cloud compliance models. The requirements for data protection, data security and data sovereignty are leading to a rethink among cloud providers and users [29].

Trustworthy and sovereign cloud solutions that meet European requirements are becoming increasingly important [30]. Regulation is therefore proving to be a driver of innovation and new business models in the cloud market.

5.2   Strategic Implications and Recommendations for Action

The regulatory developments have strategic implications for European cloud providers. In order to remain competitive, they must develop cloud solutions that meet the requirements for data protection and data sovereignty [31]. In doing so, they should rely on technical foundations such as encryption, location truth, audit trails and open standards.

It is also advisable to participate in European initiatives such as GAIA-X and enter into partnerships with other trustworthy providers. By clearly positioning themselves as an European alternative to the major US providers, they can develop unique selling points and benefit from the regulatory framework.

5.3   Need for Further Research and Open Questions

Despite the promising developments in the area of cloud sovereignty, there is still a need for further research. On the one hand, technical solutions need to be further improved in order to meet the requirements for security, transparency and interoperability. On the other hand, the legal framework needs to be further developed and adapted to the new technological possibilities. This raises questions about the liability of cloud providers, the enforcement of data protection rights and the drafting of contracts [32].

Future studies should focus more on the human and social aspects, such as knowledge, trust, acceptance or user behavior in the context of cloud and digital sovereignty. It is also important to further investigate the role and responsibility of various stakeholders such as cloud providers, companies, employees, and regulators.

Overall, it is clear that cloud sovereignty is not just a compliance issue, but also offers considerable business potential. European cloud providers have the opportunity to differentiate themselves in the market with trustworthy and legally compliant solutions and to benefit from regulatory developments. In recent years, the European Union has adopted a comprehensive package of regulations for the digital economy. European cloud providers can and should take advantage of this.

References

1. Albrecht, J.P.: How the GDPR will change the world. Eur. Data Prot. Law Rev. **2**, 287–289 (2016)
2. Daskal, J.: Microsoft Ireland, the CLOUD Act, and International Lawmaking 2.0. (2018)
3. Voigt, P., Von dem Bussche, A.: The EU general data protection regulation (GDPR). Springer, Cham (2017). https://doi.org/10.1007/978-3-319-57959-7
4. Hummel, P., Braun, M., Tretter, M., Dabrock, P.: Data Sovereignty: A Review. Big Data Soc. **8** (2021)
5. Christakis, T.: "European Digital Sovereignty": Successfully Navigating Between the "Brussels Effect" and Europe's Quest for Strategic Autonomy (2020)
6. Tankard, C.: What the GDPR means for businesses. Netw. Secur. **2016**, 5–8 (2016)
7. European Commission: Data Act: Proposal for a Regulation on harmonised rules on fair access to and use of data (2022)
8. Blancato, F.G.: The cloud sovereignty nexus: how the European Union seeks to reverse strategic dependencies in its digital ecosystem. Policy Internet, 1–21 (2023). https://doi.org/10.1002/poi3.358

9. Court of Justice of the European Union: Judgment of the Court (Grand Chamber) of 16 July 2020, Data Protection Commissioner v Facebook Ireland Limited and Maximillian Schrems, Case C-311/18 (2020)
10. European Commission: EU-US Data Privacy Framework (2023)
11. Deutscher Bundestag, Wissenschaftliche Dienste: Herausgabepflichten von Daten und Informationen an US-amerikanische Sicherheitsbehörden (2024)
12. Braud, A., Fromentoux, G., Radier, B., Le Grand, O.: The road to European digital sovereignty with Gaia-X and IDSA. IEEE Network **35**, 4–5 (2021)
13. Urban, M., Garloff, K.: Sovereign cloud stack **46**, 616–621 (2022). https://doi.org/10.1007/s11623-022-1669-5
14. Irwin, A., Ungar, D.: Digital sovereignty and governance in the data economy: data trusteeship instead of property rights on data (2023). https://doi.org/10.1007/978-3-662-65974-8_15
15. T-Systems International GmbH: Public Cloud IM öffentlichen Sektor. https://cloud.telekom.de/de/resource/open-telekom-cloud-whitepaper-public-sector
16. Warsmann, J.-L., Latombe, P.: Rapport d'information parla Mission d'information sur le théme "Bâtir et promouvoir une souverainetè numèrique nationale et europèenne" (2021)
17. Nextcloud GmbH: Nextcloud Solution Architecture (2018)
18. Esayas, S.Y.: A walk into the cloud and cloudy it remains: the challenges and prospects of 'processing' and 'transferring' personal data. Comput. Law Secur. Rev. **28**, 662–678 (2012). https://doi.org/10.1016/j.clsr.2012.09.007
19. Johnston, M.P.: Secondary data analysis: a method of which the time has come. Qual. Quant. Methods Libr. **3**, 619–626 (2017)
20. Smith, E.: Using Secondary Data in Educational and Social Research. McGraw-Hill Education (UK) (2008)
21. IDC: IDC Forecasts Worldwide Public Cloud Services Spending to Reach $1.35 Trillion in 2027 (2023)
22. Research and Markets: Global Cloud Infrastructure Services Market (2023–2028) Competitive Analysis, Impact of Economic Slowdown & Impending Recession, Ansoff Analysis (2024)
23. Gartner: Forecast: Public Cloud Services, Worldwide, 2021–2027, 4Q23 Update (2023)
24. Lundborg, M., Gull, I., Baischew, D.: Strategische Bedeutung von Cloud-Diensten für die digitale Souveränität von KMU. Teil 1 - Marktübersicht Cloud-Anbieter (2022)
25. PwC: How businesses will unlock the transformational power of cloud: PwC EMEA Cloud Business Survey 2023. https://www.pwc.com/gx/en/issues/technology/cloud-business-survey.pdf
26. Joshua, S., Gans, J., Mikaël, H.: Economic analysis of proposed regulations of cloud services in Europe. Eur. Competition J. **1**, 1–47 (2023). https://doi.org/10.1080/17441056.2023.2228668
27. Capgemini Research Institute: The Journey to Cloud Sovereignty: Assessing Cloud Potential to Drive Transformation and Build Trust (2022)
28. Synergy Research Group: Cloud Market Gets its Mojo Back; AI Helps Push Q4 Increase in Cloud Spending to New Highs. https://www.srgresearch.com/articles/cloud-market-gets-its-mojo-back-q4-increase-in-cloud-spending-reaches-new-highs. Accessed 23 May 2024
29. Ali, M., Khan, S.U., Vasilakos, A.V.: Security in cloud computing: opportunities and challenges. In: Information Sciences, pp. 357–383. Elsevier (2015)
30. Tamburri, D.A.: Design principles for the General Data Protection Regulation (GDPR): a formal concept analysis and its evaluation. Inf. Syst. **91**, 101469–101470 (2020)
31. Alruwaili, F.F., Gulliver, T.A.: Secure migration to compliant cloud services: a case study. J. Inf. Secur. Appl., 50–64 (2018)
32. Djemame, K., Armstrong, D., Guitart, J., Macias, M.: A risk assessment framework for cloud computing. IEEE Trans. Cloud Comput. **4**, 265–278 (2014)

Author Index